Collective Bargaining
in Higher Education

ACRL Publications in Librarianship no. 38

Collective Bargaining in Higher Education:
Its Implications for Governance and Faculty Status for Librarians

Proceedings of a Preconference Institute Sponsored by

ACADEMIC STATUS COMMITTEE
ASSOCIATION OF COLLEGE AND RESEARCH LIBRARIES

at San Francisco, June 27 and 28, 1975

Edited by

MILLICENT D. ABELL

American Library Association

Chicago 1976

Association of College and Research Libraries
Publications in Librarianship

Library of Congress Cataloging in Publication Data

Main entry under title:

Collective bargaining in higher education.

(ACRL publications in librarianship ; no. 38)
Bibliography: p.

    1.   Collective bargaining—College librarians—United
States—Congresses.   2.   College librarians—United
States—Faculty status—Congresses.   I.   Abell,
Millicent D.   II.   Association of College and Research
Libraries.   Committee on Academic Status.   III.   Se-
ries: Association of College and Research Libraries.
ACRL publications in librarianship ; no. 38.

Z674.A75   no. 38   [Z675.U5]   020'.8s   [331.89'041'02770973]
ISBN 0-8389-3189-8   76-51403

Contents

Preface

In his introduction to this volume James Schmidt concisely describes the genesis of the Preconference Institute and its relevance to the work of the Academic Status Committee of the Association of College and Research Libraries (ACRL). In planning the Preconference Institute the committee had two principal purposes. The first was to assist librarians in the understanding and evaluation of collective-bargaining issues by providing participants with information on the nature of collective bargaining and its influence on governance in higher education, on objectives of various collective-bargaining agents, and on academic library experiences with collective bargaining. The second purpose was to assist the Academic Status Committee in the development of new materials and programs on the issues of governance and status that can be disseminated to the profession at large. These proceedings represent one of the attempts to accomplish this objective.

As is usually the case, the collective-bargaining knowledge and experience of the participants varied widely. To provide a modest foundation of knowledge of the relevant terminology and issues, orientation materials were provided in advance of the Institute. Some of these background papers proved to be so valuable to the participants that the originals or updated revisions have been reproduced in this volume.

The original papers are arranged in the same order in which they were presented over the one and one-half days of the Institute. Because of redundancies, the exchanges with the audience, particularly those following the panel presentations, have been extensively edited and reordered.

The first two speakers, Donald Wollett and Kenneth Mortimer, were asked, as researchers in collective bargaining and governance in higher education, to describe the issues from a broad perspective. Wollett compares the characteristics of traditional governance systems with the characteristics of collective-bargaining systems and identifies areas of contrast and potential conflict between the two. Mortimer deals with the extent and patterns of faculty bargaining and examines the roles of faculty senates and students in relation to bargaining.

Panel members who represented the three major academic bargaining associations were asked to discuss their problems, priorities, and strategies with regard to achieving status gains for librarians as well as their particular concerns regarding status issues for faculty generally. Dirck Brown of the National Education Association (NEA) stresses that group's position on procedural due process, a set of issues of increasing importance as fiscal resources for higher education decline. Charles McClain traces the activity of the American Association of University Professors (AAUP) in governance and in collective bargaining and describes some significant contractual arrangements. Warren Kessler, representing the American Federation of Teachers (AFT), explores the questions whether librarians as professionals need unions and whether one union is more appropriate than another.

The fourth panel participant, David Feller, was asked to describe the Berkeley Faculty Association, a model of organization with which many librarians must become familiar in order to define their own roles and strategies on campuses where such associations exist. The fifth member of the panel, Daniel Orr, was asked to present a quite different and critically important perspective on collective bargaining in higher education. He challenges some assumptions about the accomplishments of unionization in society at large and examines the prospects for unionization to be beneficial in an academic setting.

Several significant themes are explored further in the panel discussion: unit determination, selection of an agent, models of collective bargaining, and achievements of unions.

To provide opportunities for a greater exchange of experiences and ideas among the Institute participants, a number of social encounters and a small group session were scheduled. Librarians who as members of professional associations, unions, or management have been particularly active in collective bargaining were asked to serve as leaders in these sessions.

The authors of the last two papers are librarians, teachers of librarians, and researchers in the field of librarianship and collective bargaining. Jean Kennelly presents the results of a survey of academic librarians' involvement in collective bargaining, especially conducted to gather information for the Institute participants. Gwen Cruzat discusses the context in which academic librarians must confront collective-bargaining issues. Included are enabling legislation, the attitude of collective-bargaining agents, institutional characteristics and faculty status, and bargaining agreement provisions for librarians.

In his Conference summary, Kenneth Mortimer explores the collective-bargaining process, examines the continuum of governance relationships, and comments on institutional characteristics, contract provisions, and the motivations for collective bargaining. He concludes with some strategic recommendations for academic librarians.

The Preconference Institute and these proceedings are the result of the ideas and effort of many people. Each of my colleagues on the Planning Committee more than once proved her or his ability to produce in crisis as well as calm. They are Mary Louise Cobb (College of William and Mary), Marjorie Dennin (Northern Virginia Community College), Joan Gotwals (University of Pennsylvania), and John Haak (University of California, San Diego). James Schmidt (SUNY at Albany), who chaired the sponsoring Academic Status Committee, met regularly with the planners and frequently made valuable contributions to our discussions. The Committee is also especially grateful for his many ideas and his suggestions to Jack Weatherford, who seems to know everybody who is interested in academic collective bargaining.

The special role and contributions of Beverly Lynch, ACRL executive secretary, must also be noted. In my experience, every working group in ACRL benefits from her advice and her logistical and moral suport. Ours was no exception.

Neither the Conference nor the proceedings would have been possible without the highly competent and hard-working local arrangements committee of Alison Howard, James Mackie, Susan Quinlan, and William Whitson, who chaired the group.

Each speaker and discussion leader was invited to participate because of her or his unique knowledge or experience in collective bargaining in higher education. The high quality of their contributions to the program and their generosity with their time and effort are gratefully acknowledged.

Millicent D. Abell
State University of
New York at Buffalo

Introduction

C. James Schmidt

C. James Schmidt is Director of Libraries at the State University of New York at Albany. He has held administrative positions in the libraries at Southwest Texas State University and Ohio State University. He is currently chairing the Academic Status Committee for a second term.

There are three purposes in my remarks: to describe how the Preconference Institute came to be, to relate its goals to the work of the Academic Status Committee, and to suggest some key issues. All are intended to create a context or frame of reference for the presentations and discussions that follow.

The idea of this Preconference Institute originated in the fall of 1973, when a few members of the Academic Status Committee met to discuss and plan a program on governance for the 1974 annual conference in New York. The major portions of that program were a videotape on governance, which is available on interlibrary loan from ACRL, and the paper on governance by Dwight Ladd, which was published in the March 1975 issue of *College and Research Libraries*. It became evident early in the planning meeting that governance was too complex a topic to cover in a two-hour program and that collective bargaining as a major force impinging on governance could and should consume a larger program.

Insofar as the Academic Status Committee is concerned, the topic of this Preconference Institute is the third component of what we on the committee characterize as implementation of the standards for faculty status. You will recall that the Standards for Faculty Status were approved by the ACRL membership in Dallas in 1971 and that the Joint Statement on Faculty Status was approved by the ACRL membership

1

in Chicago in 1972 and by AAUP in 1973. Taking these two basic documents as our policy statements on this matter, the Academic Status Committee has since focused on what we would characterize as implementation. We published a model statement of criteria and procedures for appointment, promotion, and tenure that was approved by the ACRL board in 1974. We presented the program on governance last year in New York; and now we have this Institute.

It is appropriate to make a few comments about our assumptions in planning this program and about a few key issues. First, we assumed that faculty status per se was not at issue but rather how collective bargaining impinges on that status. If you have faculty status, does collective bargaining enhance it? If you do not have it, does collective bargaining help or hinder getting it?

Second, the Institute was not intended to advocate collective bargaining but rather to present information about it and to provide an opportunity to discuss issues, share experiences, and analyze questions.

Third, the fundamental principle underlying the entire work of the Academic Status Committee, going back to the committee's conception in 1959 or thereabouts, was explicit throughout the planning process for the Institute: librarians should be fully identified with other faculty on the campus. Therefore, if collective bargaining exists for faculty, then it ought to exist on the same terms for library faculty.

It is worth noting that the history of collective bargaining in higher education is rather short. The first major contract in higher education was signed in the late sixties. To date, contracts cover approximately 15 percent of the faculty in higher education and about 10 percent of the institutions of higher education.

There are a few key issues that I see in collective bargaining. The first can only be characterized as the jurisdictional morass. You are either under the National Labor Relations Board or you are not: if you are in private higher education, you are; if you are not in private higher education, you may be under a state agency—but not every state has an agency and every state which has an agency does not have the same kind of agency, because all state laws are not the same. There is a rather complex range of questions that pertain to jurisdiction.

The second key issue, and the central one for academic librarians, is the definition of the bargaining unit: Who is in it, who is not in it, and who is in it with you? There are, it seems to me, two dimensions to this definition, one horizontal and the other vertical. The horizontal dimension is Who is in the unit with particular reference to those categories of people outside the library? Are the librarians in the unit with other faculty? What about other people on the campus, such as counselors and the like, and the whole range of professional people who work in your administration building doing accounting and purchasing?

The vertical dimension is particularly crucial and is internal to the library. It is in this dimension that the issue of who the supervisor is arises. The question Who is the supervisor, who is management? requires a rather complex legal definition, based on the National Labor Relations Act. In higher education the distinction between supervisor and non-supervisor is less clear than in a typical corporate environment.

The third issue in collective bargaining is the choice of the bargaining agent. There will be presentations about the range of alternatives that are available, from no agent, to an agent with any of several national affiliations, to someone in the middle of that continuum: an agent who is local, independent, and not affiliated with one of the national organizations that are active in bargaining in higher education.

The fourth issue, which I would call to your attention but not explore in detail, is consequences. What are the consequences of collective bargaining in terms of the organizational structure of libraries? What is the impact of collective bargaining on patterns of service, on the nature of the service, on the hours of the service, on the composition of the personnel to provide the services?

Finally, what are the implications of collective bargaining for the fiscal crunch into which we are moving in higher education? Kenneth Boulding, in a paper he presented in the fall of 1974, referred to the future of higher education as the management of decline. We are faced with decline in resources, decline in enrollment, and decline in a number of other respects. What, then, are the consequences of collective bargaining for the management of decline?

The Nature of Collective Bargaining and Its Relationship to Governance in Higher Education

Donald H. Wollett

Donald H. Wollett is Director of Employee Relations for the state of New York. He has practiced law in Seattle and New York City and has served on the law faculties of the University of Washington, New York University, Louisiana State University, and the University of California, Davis. He has also been an arbitrator and has written numerous books and articles on labor relations.

In order to discuss collective bargaining and its relationship to governance it is necessary to define a governance system and then a collective-bargaining system. Only then can the two be compared, with areas of contrast and tension highlighted. When that has been done, the choices between these two systems can be discussed intelligently.

Although the characteristics of governance systems may vary, their basic components are standard and uniform: the governing body of the institution, the administration (including the president), and the employed staff. The staff may be divided into two broad categories, professional and nonprofessional. With these components in mind, we can turn to characteristics.

First, governance usually depends upon shared authority. This means that the governing body, which is the legal depository of authority to run the institution, shares its authority with the administration and with some of the members of the staff.

A second characteristic of a governance system is that the governing board has the power to recall authority when it deems this to be appropriate. It is important to understand this point because it affords a significant contrast with a collective-bargaining system. In a governance system the governing body shares power with the administration, the

4

faculty, and the librarians (and whatever other staff may be involved) by choice, not by legal compulsion. If the governing board elects to withdraw such authority, there is ordinarily no effective legal recourse on the part of those who previously enjoyed the sharing experience. In a bargaining system, power is redistributed pursuant to a legally enforceable instrument: the collective agreement.

A third characteristic is that a governance system is limited to the "community of scholars." (According to Dwight Ladd, the existence of such a community is a myth.[1] Nonetheless, belief in its existence persists.) This means that some parts of the institutional work force are excluded from participation: the entire nonprofessional staff, adjunct lecturers and professors, most or all nonteaching professionals, and the supportive staff, such as registrars, placement officers, counselors, and librarians. Some librarians may participate if they also have faculty status and are on the tenure track. The important point is that, in contrast with collective bargaining and collective-bargaining units in higher education, participation in governance systems is typically narrowly based.

A fourth characteristic of governance is the broad scope of matters dealt with: salary levels, fringe benefits, allocations of money (whether a salary increase is to be distributed according to merit or across the board), salary administration, appointments, promotions, job security (tenure), admission, tuition and fees, programs, curriculum, degree requirements, staffing patterns, and workload. All of these subjects (and others) are usually encompassed in a governance system. A collective-bargaining system typically deals with a much narrower range of subjects.

A fifth characteristic of governance systems is the diffuse nature of decision making.[2] The University of California affords a good example of this phenomenon. At that nine-campus system there is a systemwide faculty council at the top of the governance structure. There are senates with an elaborate committee structure on each campus, beneath which are the faculties of each college or school. Paralleling this governance structure is a management establishment, consisting of the central administration, the deans, and department chairmen.

Its governance and management structures are connected at all levels by a network of liaison arrangements. To identify who decides what in a real (as distinguished from a formal) sense is challenging and sometimes frustrating. The faculty at the "grass roots" level, working through

1. Dwight R. Ladd, "Myths and Realities of University Governance," *College and Research Libraries* 36:97–105 (March 1975).
2. The locus-of-authority spectrum runs from the faculty-autonomy-residual-administration-veto model to the administration-autonomy-faculty-manipulation model. The latter need not concern us because it is basically a style of authoritarian management which has only the trappings of governance.

faculty committees, appears to have effective authority over matters such as curriculum, as well as—subject to review by the senate committee and veto by the administration—appointments, promotions, and tenure acquisition or denial. On the other hand, the deans and department chairmen initiate and control—subject to collegial review and higher administrative approval—matters such as step increases. Here the faculty seemingly has influence but not authority.

In many other matters the faculty appears to have, at best, a muted voice—in course assignments, office space, hours of instruction—although it may be able to bring about the downfall of a department head or a dean who incurs collegial disfavor. Some matters which are the central concern of a collective-bargaining system—overall salary adjustments and improvements in fringe benefits—are formally covered but really untouched by governance systems.

There are two noteworthy aspects of this system for decision making. First, the difficulty in identifying who decides what in an authoritative sense makes it hard (or impossible) to hold a particular person accountable for anything. Second, the fact that there is an employer-employee relationship—with a management cadre separate and distinct from those who are managed—is blurred. There are many matters the employees manage themselves (as well as other employees). Moreover, the members of the formal managerial corps may appear to be as responsive to those they ostensibly manage as they are to the employing entity.

Finally, governance systems are fiscally dependent. Their operational funds come from institutional sources or, in a publicly funded college or university, from the public purse. This means that the ability of a governance system to function is controlled by external forces. For example, in New York in 1969 the state comptroller refused to permit the faculty senate of the State University of New York to pay any of the fees owed to a law firm that had handled its collective-bargaining activities. He vetoed the power of the senate to expend budgeted funds.

Now to the components of a collective-bargaining system. There is an identifiable management which is accountable internally to students and externally to funding sources, such as parents and donors in private institutions and taxpayers and politicians in public ones. Collective bargaining is a two-party adversarial system, with management on one side, the organizational representative of the employees on the other.

The organizational representatives of the employees are selected by the members of discrete voting groups, called *appropriate bargaining units*. Bargaining units in higher education are typically broad based (much broader than the so-called community of scholars) and include tenure-track faculty, nonteaching professionals, librarians, counselors, placement officers, registrars, and sometimes even adjunct professors.

The other characteristics of collective bargaining are multifarious and in sharp contrast with governance. First, the concept of shared authority is essentially alien to collective bargaining. At the threshhold of negotiations—when the parties start from scratch—management has the ultimate authority to manage and the bargaining representative has only the authority to bargain. Representatives of management and representatives of the union negotiate with each other over the rules which will govern the terms and conditions of employment. What comes out of the process is a legal instrument, called a *collective-bargaining agreement,* which restricts management's power to make decisions and creates legal rights that are enforceable by the union, and in some instances by individual members of the bargaining unit. Management does not share its authority conditionally, as it does in a governance system. Rather than reserve the right to recall authority, it gives up some of that authority for a specified term.

For instance, if there is a commitment in the collective-bargaining agreement to raise salaries 7 percent at the beginning of the second academic year, that promise has to be honored. It is a contractual obligation which has to be met. The same is true with respect to a commitment to improve fringe benefits or a provision specifying that faculty on the tenure ladder shall not be denied tenure without good and sufficient cause. A collective-bargaining agreement is an enforceable contract, either in court or in arbitration.

Second, in one sense the subjects of collective bargaining are narrower in scope than they are in governance; in another sense, broader. Programs, curricula, admission requirements, grading standards, selecting deans and department heads, hiring, and degree requirements, which are dealt with in governance, are typically not subject to the bargaining process, nor are they covered by the terms of the collective-bargaining agreement. On the other hand, salary and fringe-benefit levels and many other terms and conditions of employment are beyond the effective reach of governance but lie at the heart of a functioning collective-bargaining system.

There are subject-matter overlaps between collective bargaining and governance, particularly with respect to personnel administration—matters such as step increases, promotions, reappointments and nonrenewals, and tenure.

Third, in collective bargaining who decides what is clear. The fact that there is an employer-employee relationship—those who manage and those who are managed—is not blurred. On the contrary, it is emphasized. In collective bargaining, management governs and the employees, through their union, react. Decisions are made and affirmed at various levels of the managerial hierarchy on matters such as appointments, promotions, step increases, nonrenewals, and conferring or denying tenure. Employees either complain, through their union, that particular decisions violate the collective-bargaining agreement or they demand that the agreement be amended to protect or advance the employee interest, which they feel has been abridged.

In governance, particularly in personnel administration, roles are obscured. Management is faculty (or vice versa). A faculty member, acting in a system of self-government, may serve on a departmental or divisional recruiting committee or a promotional or tenure committee. He or she may also be part of a senate structure and have so much managerial responsibility that released time from the classroom is needed. The decisions are managerial in the sense that they involve direction and control, and sometimes termination of the on-the-job life of other employees. An aggrieved person, for instance a teacher denied tenure, may find, if he or she is able to fix responsibility, that it lies with colleagues, not with the administration. Indeed, the individual may discover that the administration is in agreement but is reluctant to clash with the governance establishment.

Fourth, it is easy to fix responsibility in collective bargaining. The union is responsible to its constituency, that is, the members of the voting unit, for policing or enforcing the collective-bargaining agreement and for periodically renegotiating its terms in order to improve salaries and fringe benefits and to reduce workloads. Accountability is established when the union leaders stand for reelection and when a renegotiated collective-bargaining agreement is submitted to the membership for ratification (or rejection) prior to implementation.

In a governance system, responsibility is obscure. To whom are participants in governance responsible? To the community of scholars? To the tenured portion of the community of scholars? To the senior portion of the tenured part? To the administration? To some mix of the two? How is accountability established? To whom must the participants in governance decisions answer? Who judges their performance and what are the consequences of an adverse judgment?

Finally, a collective-bargaining system is self-sustaining. The union is independent, free of reliance on institutional support.[3] It is separately funded by membership dues.

---

3. The employer may agree to some subsidization of union activities; e.g., shop stewards or their academic analogues may get released time to investigate grievances. But this support is not vital to the system. If it were terminated, the organization could continue to perform its functions with funds from its own treasury.

What is the choice for librarians? Should they seek greater involvement in existing governance systems? Or creation of a governance system of their own? Or should they opt for collective bargaining?

The first choice—greater involvement in existing governance systems—would have the obvious disadvantages which afflict minority groups in any political system where the legitimacy of their full participation is not accepted by the majority. This situation exists because the systems are operated by and for elite academic groups, namely, tenure-track faculties.

Creation of a governance system by and for librarians would not improve the situation. Indeed, it might make it worse. Librarians are a smaller percentage of the total academic work force than tenure-track faculty. They would continue to be in a disadvantaged competitive position vis-à-vis the faculty, particularly since most of the administrators with whom they would do business are former faculty members. Very few are ex-librarians.

If the primary objective of librarians is improvement of salaries, fringe benefits, and working conditions, collective bargaining is an appealing alternative. However, there are a number of problems and difficulties with this choice.

First, collective bargaining costs money. The system will not work unless a very large majority of the members of the voting and bargaining unit join the organization and pay membership dues and fees.

Second, collective bargaining, if it is to work, requires a massive expenditure of time and energy by employee participants.

Third, the voting and bargaining units, if collective bargaining for librarians is to be effective, should include more than professional librarians. Ideally, the entire library operation and all its personnel should be encompassed in a broad-based unit.

The reasons for this third conclusion lie in an analysis of what makes collective bargaining tick. It works because the governing body and its agents are impelled to negotiate, reach for compromises, and seek agreements by fear of the consequences of the failure to do so, which usually means some form of *job action* by the employees. If, in the public sector, the service interrupted or disturbed by job action is of direct value to consumers who have political clout vis-à-vis the college or university decision makers, a strike may be effective.

Ironically, however, the teaching and research functions of a college or university ordinarily can be disturbed without generating significant political pressures. Interruption of the teaching service or the investigative function does not seem to create terror in the hearts of legislators or governing boards, except perhaps a threatened strike of a teaching hospital which provides services to a community.[4] This is why most teacher strikes in publicly funded higher education (junior colleges excepted) have failed to produce much for the strikers. However, librarians serve not only students but members of the larger community. Thus an interruption or curtailment of library service has a wider impact.[5]

Nevertheless, job action by professional librarians alone would probably not be effective, either because they would not be missed much in the short run or because their functions could be backstopped because of the relatively small numbers involved. But if *all* library personnel engage in concerted activity, management has a much more difficult time maintaining service.

Thus it seems probable that collective bargaining for professional librarians is most likely to be effective if they are part of a broad unit, consisting of all library employees or, alternatively, embracing other college or university employees who perform service functions for the community. The disadvantage to professional librarians of inclusion in such broad units is that they will be part of a minority group. Anne Commerton has written of this feeling among librarians who are part of the professional-staff bargaining unit of the State University of New York. Librarians may feel that their interests have sometimes been sacrificed to the advantage of the majority in the 16,000-member unit.[6]

Another option for librarians is to become part of or to establish a governance system for the protection and advancement of professional concerns while seeking collective bargaining for bread-and-butter matters. However, there are so many tensions between these two systems that their coexistence would be very difficult if not impossible.[7] Nevertheless, governance systems have continued to function even where higher-education faculty have opted for collective bargaining, and apparently with about the same effectiveness or ineffectiveness they had prior to the establishment of a bargaining system.

4. In contrast, since quality students who can pay the costs are scarce, *private* colleges and universities may find that a credible strike threat is a significant motivation.

5. Compare the effectiveness of strikes in K–12 public school systems, which perform the custodial function of baby-sitting, the interruption of which *does* generate political pressure on decision makers.

6. Anne Commerton, "Union or Professional Organization? A Librarian's Dilemma," *College and Research Libraries* 36: 129–35 (March 1975).

7. Donald H. Wollett, "Self-Governance and Collective Bargaining for Higher Education Faculty: Can the Two Systems Co-Exist?" in Judith P. Vladeck and Stephen C. Vladeck, eds., *Collective Bargaining in Higher Education—The Developing Law* (New York: Practising Law Institute, 1975), p. 33–51.

AUDIENCE EXCHANGE WITH DONALD H. WOLLETT

Audience: What is the impact of right-to-work laws on collective bargaining?

Wollett: Right-to-work laws are significant only with respect to the legality of what is called the *union security arrangement*, in which employment is linked to support of the union or the organization either by membership or by requiring that a service fee be paid as a condition of employment. If the state has a right-to-work statute, even though in terms not applicable to public employment, the courts in that state would probably say that the public policy which is manifested by that right-to-work statute is such that union security arrangements, as I defined them, are not permissible. They are illegal.

Audience: In describing the governance system, you spoke of faculty sharing in management functions through committees. What happens in collective-bargaining situations? Does the faculty have no role in tenure or other managerial decisions within the department?

Wollett: I would not say that the faculty has no role. In some of the systems, as they now operate, the faculty, the departmental faculty, has continued its traditional role. There is the anomalous situation where the aggrieved person who is denied tenure is really complaining not about the decision of the administration but the decision of his colleagues. If that grievance is to go to arbitration, the only way the administration can avoid arbitration is to reverse the faculty determination. If the administration affirms the determination, with which it may disagree, then the matter may go to arbitration under some contracts. That, it seems to me, would be very awkward. I do not know how to reconcile the collective-bargaining system and the self-governing system in that kind of situation. However, it illustrates that even under collective-bargaining systems, as at the City University of New York, the faculty continues to have a significant voice in decisions of that sort.

Audience: Librarians are defining themselves in relation not only to classroom faculty but to library support staff as well. What role have clerical and other nonprofessional people taken in collective bargaining at SUNY [State University of New York]?

Wollett: There is a unit structure in the state of New York which is unique. SUNY has a bargaining unit, a professional staff unit which encompasses a wide range of professional employees of the State University of New York. Most of the nonprofessional people are part of other bargaining units and are represented by the Civil Service Employees Association and Council 82 of AFSCME, which negotiate separately.

Audience: Is union security, such as an agency shop, possible in SUNY?

Wollett: No. There seems to be general agreement, with which I concur, that agency shops under the law of New York, as it presently exists, are illegal. There are, however, several bills in the state legislature to permit agency shops.

Audience: Is it not likely that faculty will be less able to participate in management in a collective-bargaining system, where the union representative speaks for the faculty, than in the governance system, where a faculty member may speak for himself in the senate or a similar body?

Wollett: Yes. At least the tenured faculty would certainly lose authority over a number of matters in which they now have considerable authority. Furthermore, they are not likely to gain much authority in terms of affecting decisions by the governing board or a legislature with respect to salary levels and fringe benefits. Thus the move to collective bargaining would probably be a loss. With respect to junior members of the faculty who are on the tenure track but are not yet tenured, it is very hard to respond to that question. The extent to which senior members of the faculty permit junior members to participate in the decision-making process varies widely. If they are permitted to participate, then the collective bargaining system probably has little to offer them, for the same reasons that it has little to offer the tenured faculty. However, in most situations, if I were a junior faculty member, I would rather take my chances with collective bargaining than with senior tenured faculty running a governance system.

Audience: What do you predict for the 1980s? Will collective bargaining prevail and all our working relationships be in an adversarial context?

Wollett: I do not want to presume to be a prophet. Frankly, I do not know that collective bargaining is going to be very meaningful in higher education. It is still an open question whether collective bargaining is going to grow very much more in higher education. There is serious question about how effective it has been where it is now established. It would be premature to say that the decade of the eighties is going to see the spread of collective bargaining to all employment areas. It must also be said that the distinction between collegial and adversarial relationships, as functions of a governance system on the one hand and a collective bargaining system on the other, seems to me to be unreal. The fact is that faculty members in governance systems frequently have interests which are quite adverse and they fight intensely with each other. In a collective-bargaining system they may direct their conflicting opinions and their anger to the administrative officer rather than engage in an adversarial relationship with each other.

Audience: You stated that, for an academic institution, a criterion for defining a bargaining unit is not a community of scholars but a community of interests. How would you apply that criterion to the library, where librarians with academic status relate to other members of the faculty and also to library staff members who do not have academic status?

Wollett: In my judgment, a faculty bargaining unit, including librarians who have faculty status, works from too narrow a base to be effective in a collective-bargaining system. It may be very effective in a governance system, but not in a collective-bargaining system, where you change relationships around. When you try to get some authority or at least exert some pressure on matters with which the governance systems really do not deal, such as salary increases and fringe benefits, I think you have to have a broader base than the tenure-track faculty, even if you include librarians with academic status. It is not realistic to expect a governance system to do much for you in those areas. It is not equipped or intended to deal effectively with a board of regents about money. It is also going to be increasingly difficult for a governance system to deal with external agencies. Legislatures and governors and offices, such as the one I direct in New York, are increasingly interested in what is going on in the university, and in issues such as tenure quotas. Governance systems are not structured to deal with my office or the legislature; collective-bargaining agents may or may not be—I am not sure yet.

Audience: You spoke about a broad-based collective-bargaining unit for the university. Could you define, in general terms, the appropriate community of interest for a university?

Wollett: I cannot generalize about that. Community of interest varies, depending on the local facts. I would think that the bargaining unit in SUNY, which is a systemwide unit and encompasses tenure-track faculty, librarians, registrars, counselors, nonteaching professionals, and so on, reflects a community of interest in that situation. That was the judgment reached by the Public Employee Relations Board after voluminous testimony and almost a year of hearings.

Audience: If the professionals are in one unit and the clerical and support staff in another unit, there would be two different representatives of the library staff, even though they have many common interests.

Wollett: Whether the clerical and the professional staff should be included in one unit depends in part upon the extent to which they can resolve their conflicts internally and present some kind of solid front to management at the bargaining table. That, I think, is what we really mean by community of interest. Is there more that holds these people together, so that they can work out their problems as a group, than divides them? If the answer to that question is yes, they ought to be in the same unit. If the answer is no, they ought to go their separate ways. That is the issue from the employees' point of view. From management's point of view—and I happen to be management right now—I would prefer to have them all in the same unit, even though they do not get along very well. But that is another subject.

A Survey of Experience in Academic Collective Bargaining

Kenneth P. Mortimer

Kenneth P. Mortimer is professor and research associate at the Center for the Study of Higher Education at the Pennsylvania State University. He has been a consultant to numerous private and governmental organizations on higher-education administrative issues. He has also written extensively on governance, collective bargaining, and the administration of higher education.

This paper is a general survey of recent developments in faculty collective bargaining. Like any survey, it suffers from an attempt to generalize about phenomena which do not arrange themselves into neat classifications. A more detailed analysis of the developments would show remarkable variability in the practices and implications of faculty bargaining in postsecondary education.

The survey first reports on the extent of collective bargaining and its projected growth in the next two or three years. The patterns of faculty bargaining in the various states are then presented and are followed by a discussion of governance, faculty senates, and collective bargaining. The final section is a summary of student involvement in the collective-bargaining process.

EXTENT OF FACULTY COLLECTIVE BARGAINING

Three major points can be made about the present and future status of collective bargaining in institutions of higher education. First, faculty collective bargaining is primarily a phenomenon of the public sector of higher education. Approximately 255 bargaining units represent about 90,000 faculty at 385 campuses across the United States. Three hundred and thirty-one (86 percent) of these campuses are public. Although two-year campuses initially dominated faculty bargaining in the public sector, there are now 107 public and 47 private four-year campuses at which faculty are represented by bargaining agents.[1]

Second, the growth of faculty collective bargaining has closely paralleled the enactment of state collective-bargaining laws. Between 1965 and 1972 the growth of faculty collective bargaining was dominated by activity in a few heavily populated and relatively industrialized states that adopted enabling legislation before 1970. By 1973 there were 161 organized institutions in Massachusetts, Michigan, New Jersey, New York, and Pennsylvania, representing 76 percent of the organized institutions in the country at that time. James Begin documented a "slowdown" in the growth of faculty collective bargaining during 1973[2]—a pattern that continued in 1974 and led some observers to predict a declining interest in the phenomenon. One of the major factors leading to the seeming loss of momentum in 1973, however, was the early proliferation of faculty bargaining units in the five states mentioned above. By early 1973, 79 percent of the 205 public institutions in these states had adopted collective bargaining, leaving little room for further growth.

Third, the enactment of new enabling laws, in states where such action appears imminent, is likely to produce a new acceleration of faculty collective bargaining in the public sector. According to the Carnegie Commission, there are approximately 1,313 public college and university campuses in the United States.[3] As noted, the faculties of 331 of these campuses, or about 25 percent of the total, are currently represented by bargaining agents.

Given the current status of legislative activity in the states, a fairly conservative projection would indicate that an additional 135 campuses will be unionized by 1978 or 1979 and that the new total will account for about one-third of the public campuses. It is possible that the figure will go as high as 230 additional campuses, for a new total of approximately 40 percent of all public campuses.[4]

1. "Collective Bargaining on Campuses," *Chronicle of Higher Education* 10:5 (9 June 1975).

2. James P. Begin, "Faculty Bargaining in 1973: A Loss of Momentum?" *Journal of the College and University Personnel Association* 25:79 (April 1974).

3. Carnegie Commission on Higher Education, *A Classification of Institutions of Higher Education* (New York: McGraw-Hill, 1973), p. 6.

4. Kenneth P. Mortimer and Mark D. Johnson, "State Institutional Relations under Faculty Collective Bargaining in Public Higher Education" (paper presented at the University of Wisconsin, Madison, May 1975), p. 3, 26.

ACTIVITY IN THE STATES

Collective bargaining in the public sector is regulated or influenced by a collage of state labor laws and/or ad hoc agreements. Some twenty to twenty-three states have statutes which permit collective bargaining for public employees and which have been interpreted to include college faculty and nonteaching professionals. In addition, some community colleges bargain under municipal statutes (e.g., Chicago city colleges) and some institutions bargain or have held elections on the basis of mutual agreements between the faculties and representatives of the governing board. Even without statutory mandates, the University of Colorado has had an election and the University of Cincinnati and Youngstown State in Ohio have agreed to bargain.

Some general observations can be made about the framework for faculty bargaining in states that have bargaining statutes. First, state bargaining laws rarely recognize college and university faculty as "special" categories of public employees, if indeed they are. If higher education is different from other public agencies, those differences, for the most part, are not reflected in statutes. (The Oregon statute has a special two-step election procedure for higher education and the Montana law has special clauses on bargainable items and student involvement in bargaining.)

Second, the structures for collective bargaining vary considerably from state to state. In three complex multicampus systems, the city and state universities of New York and the University of Hawaii, the faculties of two- and four-year colleges are combined into one bargaining unit. In Pennsylvania, New Jersey, Massachusetts, Minnesota, Vermont, and other states, the higher-education system is divided into separate segments and each handles bargaining activity separately. (In a few states, e.g., Massachusetts and Montana, negotiations are on a campus-by-campus basis.) Massachusetts and Pennsylvania provide good examples of variability in bargaining units.

In Massachusetts, higher education is controlled by five different governing boards: the University of Massachusetts Board, which controls three campuses; the Massachusetts State College Board of Trustees, which governs an eleven-campus system; the Massachusetts Board of Regional and Community Colleges, which governs a fifteen-campus system; the Board of Southeastern Massachusetts University; and the Board of Lowell Technological Institute, which will merge with Lowell State College in 1976 to form Lowell University. Each of these governing boards is responsible for negotiating contracts with its faculty, should the faculty choose to bargain collectively.

Up to 1974, the State College Board negotiated on a campus-by-campus basis with eight of eleven campuses. During the current [1975] negotiations, the board negotiates all items on a campus-by-campus basis, with four faculties represented by the NEA, and on a two-tier basis, with three faculties represented by AFT. The Community College Board is currently in unit hearings to determine whether it will have to continue to negotiate on a campus-by-campus basis with the faculties at three colleges or whether there will be one systemwide unit.

In Pennsylvania, the public higher-education system is divided into three sectors. There are four state-related universities: Lincoln University, Pennsylvania State University, Temple University, and the University of Pittsburgh. Each governing board has the authority to negotiate contracts and to make whatever financial agreements are required. To date, only Temple and Lincoln have dealt with their faculties collectively, although the University of Pittsburgh will probably have an election in the next year. Both Lincoln and Temple have made agreements which are legally binding on them, whether or not the legislature appropriates sufficient funds. Both Penn State and the University of Pittsburgh have resisted petitions to split branch campuses from the main campus in order to hold separate elections.

The second major sector in Pennsylvania is the state-owned colleges and Indiana University of Pennsylvania. These fourteen campuses have a board, the State College and University Board of Directors, but the essential elements of control rest with the Pennsylvania Department of Education. The department is responsible for line-item analysis of college budgets and for negotiating one collective bargaining agreement for the faculties of all the fourteen campuses.

The third sector of higher education in Pennsylvania is the fourteen community colleges. Each college has authority to negotiate with its faculty and arrive at agreements which are funded by their sponsoring school districts or local boards. The faculty at eleven of the fourteen colleges have chosen an agent. This separate-sector bargaining appears to be the dominant pattern and will probably be the pattern in California, Illinois, and Connecticut should legislation be passed in those states.

The structure for collective bargaining in Michigan constitutes a third category. The universities in that state were chartered with a high degree of autonomy and, consequently, there is no centralized bargaining structure in Michigan. Representatives of the board for each institution negotiate their agreements with faculty and present their budgets directly to the legislature.

A fourth structural category for collective bargaining occurs in Rhode Island. Its negotiations are centralized but the faculty of each institution is organized as a separate bargaining unit. University of Rhode Island faculty are represented by the American Association of University Professors, Rhode Island College faculty are represented by the American Federation of Teachers, and a National Education Association affiliate represents the faculty of Rhode Island Junior College. The chief negotiator for management is the chief of personnel for the Rhode Island Board of Regents. In this case, as in the others discussed above, collective-bargaining relationships between the institutions and the state are closely related to the relationships that existed before bargaining.

Finally, there appears to be a dominant pattern, in the multicampus setting, to include all campuses in the system in the same bargaining unit. The exceptions appear to be Massachusetts, Rhode Island, Kansas, Oregon, and Montana.

A third general observation is that there is considerable variability in state statutes as to what may be included or excluded from bargaining. Some of this language is mandatory, as in clauses that prohibit bargaining over various civil service regulations. Much of it, however, is permissive, as is the language in most *management rights* clauses, which *allow* managers to exclude certain "inherent managerial prerogatives" from the scope of bargaining but do not *force* them to do so.

Fourth, the failure to exclude traditional governance mechanisms from bargaining has raised the possibility that faculty senates and other traditional governance mechanisms are company unions and are therefore illegal. I will return to this point when I discuss senates.

Finally, collective bargaining introduces a potentially important set of new actors and provides a framework for a redistribution of authority and responsibility among the traditional actors in academic governance. In addition to members of state labor relations boards, the new actors are union officials, arbitrators, mediators, and various state administration labor relations officials. Most (if not all) of these individuals operate from the same set of assumptions about labor relations, their primary experiences are not with education, and they represent an important new policymaking constituency whose bases of operation are external to academic institutions.

Particularly in the early stages of collective bargaining, when labor relations expertise is at a premium, these new actors play an important part in shaping the collective-bargaining relationship in the governance of higher education.

GOVERNANCE AND COLLECTIVE BARGAINING

To the extent that contracts go beyond wages, fringe benefits, and faculty perquisites, they enter the realm of governance. One of the basic reasons why governance and collective bargaining are such a volatile issue in higher education is the tradition which dictates that faculty have a major role in what many industrial concerns call *management functions*, namely, planning, staffing, and quality control. In addition, the basic functions and missions of the institution are in the hands of faculty, whose professional judgment is crucial to their effectiveness.

Governance in collective-bargaining contracts takes many forms. Approximately 25 percent of the contracts in effect in higher education have some provision for the formation of joint faculty-administrative committees to handle a variety of issues. A typical clause would read as follows:

> The presently constituted organization of the university [e.g., the university senate, faculty councils, departmental personnel and budget committees] or any other or similar body composed in whole or in part of the faculty, shall continue to function at the university, provided that the action thereof may not directly or indirectly repeal, rescind, or otherwise modify the terms and conditions of this agreement.

Or:

> The board and the bargaining unit agree on the desirability of involving the faculty in formulation of college policies. This shall be accomplished at every practicable level. A guiding principle in this process is that those affected by a policy, including the community, shall have a proportional voice in the development of that policy. A formal part of this procedure will be the establishment of joint faculty-administration committees.

In conjunction with faculty participation in governance clauses, it is customary to have a management rights clause in contracts. Two studies have shown that between 68 and 75 percent of all contracts have such a clause,[5] which might read as follows:

> Nothing in this agreement shall derogate from or impair any power, right, or duty heretofore possessed by the board or by the administration except where such right, power, or duty is specifically limited by this agreement.

To my knowledge, there are no studies which identify the extent of contractual obligation by administrators and faculty for joint involvement in such matters as the selection of department chairmen, deans,

5. Margaret K. Chandler and Connie Chiang, "Management Rights Issues in Collective Bargaining in Higher Education," in Maurice C. Benewitz, ed., *Proceedings, First Annual Conference* (New York: National Center for the Study of Collective Bargaining in Higher Education, 1973), p. 58–66. Harold I. Goodwin and John O. Andes, *Collective Bargaining in Higher Education: Contract Content —1972* (Morgantown: West Virginia University Department of Educational Administration, 1973), p. 101.

and presidents. Individual contracts, of course, may guarantee faculty participation in such matters.

Although management rights clauses and provision for faculty involvement in governance are important, the major national debate concerning the impact of collective bargaining on faculty participation in governance centers on the relations which have developed or will develop between academic senates and unions.

SENATES AND COLLECTIVE BARGAINING

The rhetoric on senates and collective bargaining is that it is very difficult for the two to coexist in a given institution. The report of the American Association of Higher Education Task Force indicated that senates are likely to atrophy in competition with external bargaining agents.[6] Thus there appears to be a widespread belief that senates and collective bargaining are contradictory rather than complementary.

Wollett indicates that, with the exception of the AAUP, comments about senates by the leaders of faculty unions are uniformly critical if not derisive.[7] Much of this commentary by faculty union leaders is directed against academic senates as the *only* voice of the faculty in universitywide affairs. For political and other reasons, faculty union advocates seldom find it feasible to oppose academic senates overtly and, instead, concentrate on revealing their weaknesses. These weaknesses include the fact that administrators are members of most faculty senates and often tend to dominate their deliberative processes and that any change in their structure has to be approved by the administration. Their financial support is derived from the administration and their actions take the form of recommendations to the administration, which can implement or ignore them at its discretion.

In research on the relationships between unions and senates under collective bargaining, Garbarino classified three types of union-senate relations: cooperative, competitive, and cooptative.[8] According to Garbarino, most observers think the most common relationship between unions and senates is cooperation or, at a minimum, coexistence. His research indicates that cooperation has been the dominant type at single-campus and main-branch institutions where administrative struc-

6. American Association for Higher Education, *Faculty Participation in Academic Governance* (Washington, D.C.: National Education Association, 1967).

7. Donald H. Wollett, "The Status and Trends of Collective Negotiations for Faculty in Higher Education," *Wisconsin Law Review* no. 1:25 (1971).

8. Joseph W. Garbarino, "Faculty Unions, Senates and Institutional Administration" (speech delivered at American Council on Education, Oct. 10, 1974).

tures are simple and unions are essentially guild unions of regular-rank faculty. Senates and unions are least cooperative and most competitive in the bargaining units of large, complex institutional systems with comprehensive unions, and these systems include most unionized faculty members. Even in these large systems (presumably the State University of New York and the City University of New York), the relations between campus senates and branches of the union are often quite cooperative.

One factor that makes such cooperation work is a natural division of labor whereby senates are most active in academic matters and unions are most active in personnel and money matters. The basic question, of course, is how long such an uneasy separation of jurisdictions can prevail. Experience with more traditional forms of faculty participation in governance indicates that this separation of jurisdictions works only as long as there is no major conflict. A cynical observer of faculty senates has characterized such a relationship:

> Given a benign administration, a relaxed political climate, a liberal community, a quiescent student body, a president uninterested in the day-to-day business of the institution, academic senates have been able to contribute meaningfully to the making of academic policy.[9]

In institutions where senates tend to compete with unions, the union is often perceived as a means for supplanting the current holders of power, who at the same time constitute the traditional senate leadership. This is most likely to occur when a union that is representing a comprehensive bargaining unit faces a faculty senate which has traditionally excluded nonteaching professionals (and others) from its membership. When faced with a choice between two representatives of the faculty, administrations usually show a clear preference for the senate version, thereby bringing latent competition to the surface.

A number of institutions have used cooptative means to resolve the senate-union dilemma. This may simplistically be identified as *collegiality by contract*. In this arrangement the primacy of the union is acknowledged and the distribution of subject matter among the various types of procedural mechanisms is negotiated between representatives of the union and the administration. The authority of the senate is preserved by specific language in the contract.

Begin, who has been studying the evolution of collective bargaining since 1969, reports:

9. Eric Solomon, *Either/Or? Both/And? Collective Bargaining and Academic Senates* (brochure of United Professors of California, May 1974).

To date, none of the four-year institutions which have been bargaining have reported that faculty senates have ceased to operate, including those institutions which have been organized the longest, for example, St. Johns University, Central Michigan University, City University of New York, State University of New York, Southeastern Massachusetts, the New Jersey State Colleges, and Rutgers University. In fact, at Central Michigan University and Rutgers University there is some feeling on the part of the administration that the senates are participating more actively in policy deliberation than before the onset of collective bargaining.[10]

In a survey of faculty collective bargaining in Pennsylvania, Gershenfeld and Mortimer found five or six institutions where the senate was dissolved after collective bargaining was adopted.[11] Only one of them was a four-year college and university. The research by Begin and by Gershenfeld and Mortimer is in the exploratory stage, however, and cannot be regarded as definitive on this matter.

The relationships between the union and the senate at various institutions indicate a growing formalization. The consensus appears to be that the growing formalization of bargaining agent–senate relationships has enhanced the development of cooperative rather than competitive relationships between these decision-making forums. Without such relationships, agreeing to refer issues to traditional forums is somewhat risky for bargaining agents because there is no guarantee that a senate, which might contain different constituencies (faculty not supporting bargaining, administrators not involved in bargaining, students and competing union organizations), will produce results which are acceptable to the bargaining agent. But by developing dual leaderships and memberships, bargaining agents are more secure and thus more willing to help preserve traditional senates.[12]

I agree with Begin when he says that senates will likely retain authority only to the extent to which they are responsive to problems. Where they fail to act, the bargaining agent is likely to take the initiative. It is clear that the *initiative* under this system lies with the union rather than with the senate.

It is evident that the type of bargaining agent–senate relationship a particular bargaining agent is willing to live with is directly related with the degree of security it feels it needs against unilateral administration deci-

10. James P. Begin, "Faculty Governance and Collective Bargaining: An Early Appraisal," *Journal of Higher Education* 45:584 (November 1974).

11. Walter J. Gershenfeld and Kenneth P. Mortimer, "Preliminary Report on Collective Bargaining in Pennsylvania" (unpublished paper, spring 1975).

12. Begin, "Faculty Governance and Collective Bargaining," p. 589.

sion making. An adversary bargaining relationship tends to intensify the need for a bargaining agent to exert more formal control over traditional senates.[13]

The evolution of collective bargaining is still in its early stages but several important principles need to be understood in judging the ultimate viability of senates under systems of collective bargaining. The most important principle is that the future role of faculty senates on matters within the scope of negotiations will be determined at the bargaining table in unionized institutions. There is no good definition of what constitutes the terms and conditions of employment, and we expect that the bargaining process will expand the existing definitions. As Brown states: "It appears that when faculties designate a union, they will be placed in an industrial relations context, rather than receive special considerations that some argue are appropriate to the educational area."[14]

Under industrial relations case law, a faculty's only authority to participate in decisions on terms and conditions of employment resides in the exclusive representative, that is, the union. For a senate to have a voice on matters within the scope of the negotiations, it must be specifically ceded by the union to the senate. The point was made earlier that the union will cede this voice to the faculty senate only so long as things go well. In times of moderate or sharp conflict, the union will find it necessary to assert its control over matters involving the terms and conditions of employment.

The scenario that is being played out relative to the competition between unions and faculty senates should come to a climax in the near future. The direction it will take will be significantly affected by cases, which now are being litigated, in which the traditional practices of senates are threatened by the application of industrial relations case law to higher education. This threat lies in three basic "facts" about senate operations: (1) the senate is an employee organization, (2) its budget is derived from administrative sources, and (3) its membership includes administrators, who would not be eligible for membership in the union.

The National Labor Relations Board has not had an opportunity to rule on whether a senate is an employee organization, but in the unit determination decision at the State University of New York, the New York State Public Employee Relations Board ruled that the senate was a labor organization, although it refused to rule on whether it received unfair assistance or was employer dominated. According to Kahn, "It

13. Ibid., p. 591.

14. Ronald C. Brown, "Professors and Unions: The Faculty Senate: An Effective Alternative to Collective Bargaining in Higher Education?" *Labor Relations in Higher Education* (New York: Practising Law Institute, 1972), p. 211.

would appear to be impossible for the National Labor Relations Board to hold that a senate is not a labor organization since a senate typically deals with the administration over terms and conditions of employment."[15] The New York state board has hinted that the proper forum for such a determination would be an unfair labor practice proceeding.

The term *labor organization* is defined in section 2(5) of the National Labor Relations Act as follows:

> The term "labor organization" means any organization of any kind or any agency or employee representation committee or plan, in which employees participate and which exists for the purpose, in whole or in part of dealing with employers concerning grievances, labor disputes, wages, rates of pay, hours of employment, or conditions of work.[16]

In my view, the precedent established by the NLRB would be of overwhelming importance in the rulings of any state labor relations board.

The stage has been set for a ruling on senates as labor organizations and the extent to which the assistance they receive from administrations is unfair. A National Education Association affiliate of Pennsylvania State University has charged the administration with "(1) financing, encouraging and dominating the university faculty senate as a company union which will engage in collective bargaining activities as the exclusive voice of the faculty in universitywide affairs . . ." and with

> (2) promising economic and other benefits to discourage its employees from exercising freedom of choice in their selection of a collective bargaining representative; and (3) reconstituting the university faculty senate as a favorite, competing alternative to the employee organization in order to convince employees that economic and other benefits can be obtained from the university without formal collective bargaining under Act 195.[17]

The real issue in this case is whether the senate gets unfair assistance from the administration and whether it is employer dominated, since it is clear that the senate is a labor organization. Typically, a senate receives substantial financial support from the administration. In the Penn State case the budget of the academic senate for the 1974/75 year was $73,000. In addition, the president has the authority to appoint up to 10 percent of the members of the senate. Another 10 percent are students.

The unfair labor practice charge has been made in the atmosphere of an anti-union campaign by the administration; so the case may not be

15. Kenneth Kahn, "The NLRB and Higher Education: The Future of Policymaking through Adjudication," *UCLA Law Review* 21:155 (October 1973).

16. Ibid., p. 147.

17. Pennsylvania Labor Relations Board *v.* Pennsylvania State University, PERAC-5083-C (28 May, 1974), attachment to charge of unfair practices, p. 1–2.

a classic test case. There is a little doubt, however, that a classic case will be presented in the near future and that the ruling will be precedent setting in terms of the future of senates.

One can take no comfort from the rulings of the National Labor Relations Board relative to the special nature of higher education. The board has consistently been confounded by the question of collegiality, for example, and has not seen fit to recognize the faculty's role in the management of the institution.

It is possible that some labor relations boards may order the disestablishment of senates as employer-dominated organizations which receive unfair assistance. Certainly it should be clear that the only legal authority under collective bargaining belongs to the union. The jurisdiction of a faculty senate on terms and conditions of employment, should it be allowed to continue, will be a subject of negotiation at the bargaining table. It is problematical whether the union will continue to support the participation of the faculty senate in matters that deal with the terms and conditions of employment.

There is another alternative for senates: they may become political tools of the unions. In the interim stages, it is quite possible that senates will be used by unions to achieve gains for faculty in areas which are not mandatory subjects of negotiation. While it is difficult to predict what such subject areas might eventually be, the future of senates under collective-bargaining systems would seem to be tied to the definition of the appropriate scope of bargaining and to the political realities of senate-union coexistence during periods of high tension.

STUDENTS AND COLLECTIVE BARGAINING

There is an increase in student activity and concern about collective bargaining, and a national Research Project on Students and Collective Bargaining is studying its impact on students, as well as the potential impact of students on the process. According to Aussieker, student involvement in collective bargaining can be classified into six types: end-run bargaining, consultation and observation, coalition bargaining, tripartite bargaining, collective bargaining over student status, and student employee bargaining.[18]

Student appeals to the appropriate governing body or the legislature are examples of end-run bargaining. In the Pennsylvania state college and university system, the student leaders at one campus appeared before the local board of trustees to argue against a tuition remission plan

18. Bill Aussieker, "Student Involvement with Collective Bargaining" (unpublished paper, 1975).

for faculty dependents and their arguments were a factor in the board's rejection of the plan. In Washington and California, student lobbyists are making determined efforts to mold collective-bargaining legislation that is sensitive to their concerns.

In some institutions students have served as observers of union and management negotiations—at CUNY, Long Island University, and some of the Massachusetts state colleges.[19] In other institutions students have formed coalitions with either the faculty or administrators. For example, at Ferris State College in Michigan a student sat on management's bargaining team. At a university in Massachusetts, student leaders forced student evaluation of instruction on the faculty bargaining team and eventually got it incorporated into the contract.

Tripartite bargaining occurs where all three parties have to ratify a final agreement. In three of the Massachusetts state colleges, students were called upon to ratify those aspects of the contract which applied to their participation in college governance.

The fifth type of student involvement is collective bargaining itself. In 1971, Chicago City College students negotiated an agreement with the board which has been incorporated into the board's rules and which, its advocates argue, has the same legal status as a contract.[20] The agreement guarantees student control over student fees, provides for student participation in college governance, and guarantees constitutional freedom and due-process rights to students.

The sixth type of student involvement in bargaining is as employees. After a strike, the University of Wisconsin Teaching Assistant Association negotiated an agreement in April 1970. (The University of Minnesota teaching assistants rejected collective bargaining in an election in the spring of 1974.) Teaching assistants are now part of the Rutgers faculty bargaining unit.

Aussieker reports that student involvement has not been extensive: "As of fall 1974, there were approximately thirty incidents of the more formal types of involvement (coalition, tripartite, student and student employee bargaining) and about seventy incidents of the more informal types (consultation or end-run bargaining)."[21] In four-year institutions, fourteen of forty-eight bargaining units reported student involvement in the negotiation or administration of the contracts; thirteen of them were in public institutions and half were of the weak tripartite bargaining type.

19. Donald E. Walters, "Do Students Have a Place in Collective Bargaining?" in Thomas Mannix, ed., *Collective Bargaining in Higher Education* (New York: Center for the Study of Collective Bargaining in Higher Education, 1974), p. 98–101.

20. Norman Swenson, "Do Students Have Any Place in Collective Bargaining?" in Mannix, ed., *Collective Bargaining in Higher Education*, p. 106–10.

21. Aussieker, "Student Involvement with Collective Bargaining," p. 17.

OTHER DEVELOPMENTS

The first sections of this paper discuss developments that are, for the most part, well documented in the professional literature or by our own research. I will conclude by citing two other developments which may be less apparent but are quite important: the centralization and homogenization of faculty personnel policies by state governments and legislatures and the unionization of middle management.

The advent of faculty collective bargaining appears to be associated with a general climate of centralized control over academic personnel policies by state executive and legislative bodies. Indeed, such centralization is part of the environment which *causes* collective bargaining. Nevertheless, it seems clear that collective bargaining in the public sector has strengthened the ties between the faculty and other public employees. The link between these two groups is so strong in some states (e.g., Hawaii, New York, Massachusetts, New Jersey, and Pennsylvania) that salaries and fringe benefits are essentially determined by negotiations between the large public employee unions and the state. Faculty employment interests are, and increasingly will be, settled in these other forums.

In several Eastern states middle management has either become part of the faculty bargaining unit or has formed its own union. The drive toward job security for these employees is strong and substantial progress has been made in the CUNY and SUNY systems. In the Pennsylvania state college and university system, however, the commonwealth has succeeded in keeping these people out of the faculty bargaining unit. In the subsequent contracts the commonwealth has frozen middle managers within the structure of their current rank and has created a new civil service–type classification for all new employees. The eventual aim is to deny faculty rank and status to these employees.

The status of middle managers has received little attention in higher education. Collective bargaining appears to be forcing renewed concern about these nonteaching professionals.

AUDIENCE EXCHANGE WITH KENNETH P. MORTIMER

Audience: Please expand on the patterns of faculty bargaining and the kinds of patterns you think likely to be adopted in states like California and Illinois.

Mortimer: Instead of following the City University of New York model, where major university centers, four-year campuses, and two-year colleges are in the same unit, the trend seems to be toward adopting the Pennsylvania and New Jersey patterns. For example, the bill that is being considered and will probably be adopted in Connecticut provides for separate-sector bargaining. That is, the University of Connecticut would bargain separately should the faculty choose to unionize, as would the state colleges as a group and the community colleges as a group. It is more difficult to predict what will happen in California, but from all indications I would guess that the University of California will not be forced into a unit with the California state college and university system.

Also relevant is the geographic question of single-campus as opposed to multicampus units. In my judgment, the overwhelming precedent in the public sector is multicampus units. There are only four or five states where bargaining is campus by campus, and in at least two states that arrangement is being reconsidered.

Audience: When you speak of middle management, of whom are you speaking?

Mortimer: Middle managers are always very difficult to define. The jargon is *NTP*, "nonteaching professionals"—that does not mean librarians, by the way. NTPs are student personnel staff, counselors, registrars, admission officers, and sometimes computer specialists. In the Pennsylvania state colleges, the entire residence hall staff is in the bargaining unit. Student personnel staff accounts for 70 or 80 percent of what I referred to as middle management.

Audience: There is some middle management in the library too. Could you give us examples from institutions that have gone into collective bargaining in the public sector, especially in the multicampus systems, of the cutoff in the library? Is the cutoff just below the director, where library staff members are included in the faculty bargaining unit?

Mortimer: It would depend on the size of the staff, but the cutoff point is somewhere around the dean or the director and his or her immediate staff. There are two or three ways to get people out of the bargaining unit if you are management, or to keep them in the unit if you are faculty. One is by managerial title. Usually the deans and assistant deans are excluded, except in the State University of New York. Another means of exclusion is to designate someone as a confidential employee. In a library, for example, if there is a personnel officer, he or she would be excluded. Those who are excluded would be a very small group. If a library staff consists of twenty persons, there might be three or four who would not be in the unit—those defined as managers or supervisors—and the rest would be in the unit by virtue of the professional librarian title.

Audience: Would you give an example, perhaps from the New York system, of how the distinction has been made?

Mortimer: I do not know what the distinction is in New York. In the Pennsylvania state colleges and universities the librarians, with very few exceptions, are in the unit.

Audience: In the State University of New York, the directors of the libraries at the four university and the two medical centers were classified management/confidential and excluded from the bargaining unit in 1972. A recently completed series of hearings before the state Public Employee Relations Board has similarly categorized the head librarians or directors of libraries at the four-year colleges in the SUNY system. They are now management/confidential and therefore out of the bargaining unit. I am not aware of any library in the SUNY system where anyone other than the chief administrative officer of the library is excluded from the bargaining unit.

Audience: In the Pennsylvania state college and university system the librarians fought very hard to be included in the bargaining unit with the faculty. Would you comment on that?

Mortimer: That is a very interesting case because it represents a significant departure from the commonwealth's normal personnel policies. It is not usual that it would allow college librarians that kind of freedom because there is a statewide unit of noncollegiate librarians. It required a specific policy decision by the state to allow the college librarians to be part of the faculty unit. The case has few precedents in public employee bargaining in Pennsylvania.

Audience: What clusters of bargainable issues have you found in your surveys and how have they expanded with the growth of collective bargaining?

Mortimer: There are four or five descriptors which categorize bargainable issues. Obviously, salaries and fringe benefits are the most common items, but there is one exception. The Merchant Marine Academy does not negotiate about money, because that is federally mandated. Under the pre-1974 statute in Massachusetts, there was no negotiation about money. It had been interpreted by the attorney general and other state officers that money was not a bargainable item under that statute. Now that has changed. The new law was passed and went into effect in July 1974.

The second most common item, of course, is the grievance procedure. About 75 percent of the grievance procedures in higher education end in binding arbitration. In other words, a dispute resolution mechanism is the second category.

The third is association rights and privileges. That is, the privileges— use of the bulletin board, an office for the association, funding for copies of the collective-bargaining agreement, released time for associa-tion officers and the like—that the employee association will have.

The fourth category is what you might call terms of employment: teaching loads, work hours, credit-hour requirements, and a variety of things like faculty office space and faculty parking.

The least common category is governance items, some of which I have spoken about. An example is provision for faculty involvement in the selection of presidents, deans, department chairmen, and so forth.

Audience: In Michigan, a heavily unionized state, we are finding that the issue of student involvement in collective bargaining is becoming more significant. The University of Michigan had a long strike in the spring of 1975 related to a graduate student employee union. The Michigan Employment Relations Commission is now investigating a petition to unionize from the student employees at Michigan State University. Would you please comment further on student involvement?

Mortimer: It is very important that we understand this issue. Students are increasingly aggressive about collective bargaining, and most tradi-tional industrial relations people cannot imagine more than a two-sided table. Students have a very effective lobby in California, I understand, and one that is seeking involvement in relevant California legislation.

There is increasing concern about student involvement in various negoti-ated matters, such as the evaluation of faculty. This is particularly true in the community college. A number of evaluation systems that are negoti-ated in the collective-bargaining agreements provide for student evaluation of teaching and other kinds of performance through questionnaires. The student instructional rating form (SIR) is widely known in community colleges and is being incorporated in collective-bargaining agreements. As part of a project we are doing for the Carnegie Commission, we visited every campus in Pennsylvania that has collective bargaining, and the number of times the SIR appeared is truly amazing. It becomes the only basis on which faculty can be measured. The assumption is that faculty can be ranked in terms of the results of these kinds of surveys and one can then determine whether they should be promoted, what their salaries should be, and so on.

Student involvement *is* increasing. They now have a national voice in Allen Shark and his operation, called the Student Project on Research and Collective Bargaining. Their state lobbies are becoming very effective.

We have recently completed some longitudinal studies of governance over a five-year span. Student involvement in those institutions that were studied has changed in that students are much less concerned about what is happening on the campus than about what is happening in the legislature and the board of regents. In the late 1960s, students were pressing for involvement in the evaluation of teaching and participation on university committees. Now their focus has changed. They want to talk to the legislature, and they are very effective in doing so. They have some very crucial issues that legislators like to hear about, such as accountability for student learning. "If the kids are not learning, why do we have colleges?" The student says, "Yeah, I'm not learning, so . . ." That has a lot of appeal when the legislature is trying to cut costs and salaries and retrench in a variety of other ways. I expect to see a great increase in the pressure students bring for involvement in bargaining.

In addition, a number of students are becoming concerned about the impact that faculty bargaining will have on their own status as teaching assistants. At Penn State, the student association has taken a position in opposition to faculty bargaining because they are afraid that any cutbacks will come at the expense of the TAs.

Audience: At the University of Michigan the opposite thing happened. Our faculty is not unionized and the graduate employee negotiation strike was of great concern to the administration and the faculty as a test case.

Mortimer: This is a new and very interesting phenomenon. The potential for lobbying and forming coalitions is really remarkable. One of the unions in one of the states we are studying is giving surreptitious support to the statewide student organization. There are two examples of that support. The union contributes financially to the student house organ and pays the publication costs. The union has also paid for buses to bring students to the state capital for demonstrations on budgets and related issues.

Thus there are some coalitions where the faculty unions have seen that their interest is tied to the student interest. Certainly they know that it is no longer a sector that can be ignored. You have to deal with the students when they have this kind of political clout and are operating in a political arena.

Audience: In the establishment of a bargaining unit, how effective have health science departments and law schools been in separating themselves from the rest of the faculty?

Mortimer: We ought to get a comprehensive view of the four or five issues in defining bargaining units. One of them is a geographic issue, that is, a multicampus unit versus single-campus units. Another issue is the definition of who is management and who is labor. A third issue is the determination of part-time versus full-time faculty and whether the former ought to be included in the unit.

Finally, there is the problem of professional schools and various titles in large, complex universities. There are questions whether law schools and medical schools, for example, should be organized separately and how successful they are in that effort. In a number of instances the law schools have stayed out of the main unit because they were actively involved in a petition. I always accuse them of not having to pay legal fees and thus being able to lobby vigorously to get themselves out of units. They have been quite successful in that regard, especially in the private sector, at Syracuse, Fordham, Columbus Law School in Washington, and other institutions.

Some of the medical faculties have also been quite effective in getting out of the main unit, especially when bargaining is organized along single-campus lines, rather than in the multicampus sector. They have been successful in arguing that their interests are quite different from those of a regular faculty; they may even have different calendars, and their salary structures are certainly different. Medical faculties and law school faculties have closer ties to the professional communities than other faculties.

These points raise issues about whether an engineering faculty can make the same arguments. When I am asked to advise members of an engineering faculty on what they should do, the only response I can make is to suggest that they go to the law faculty and ask them.

Alternative Organizational Approaches to Economic, Governance, and Status Issues

PANEL PRESENTATIONS

Dirck Brown

Dirck Brown is an organizational specialist with the National Education Association (NEA). He has been with NEA for ten years as an organizer, consultant, and troubleshooter. His academic training is in education and psychology. Dr. Brown has served on the staff and faculty of the University of Iowa and the University of Denver. At the latter institution he was dean of students.

At the outset, let me state briefly that it is NEA's position that librarians should be accorded status which is equivalent to and on a parity with teaching faculty and that there should be equality both in professional status and compensation. I can best state NEA's position on these issues by commenting on its record in due process and tenure, which I want to go into in some detail. I assume that librarians will be part of the faculty bargaining unit and will, through the negotiation process, achieve parity with the faculty. Therefore the critical factor for all members of the unit, teaching faculty and librarians alike, is the protection of their professional rights.

For years the NEA and its state affiliates have been seeking legislation and court rulings which will guarantee all staff members of educational institutions the right to substantive and procedural due process. That is, however, a long-term proposition and is largely dependent on the attitude of legislators and judges. In NEA's view, a quicker and more effective method of securing these rights on an individual institution basis is collective bargaining. That process has already been described in considerable detail.

The system of collective bargaining, in NEA's view, offers the best possibility of securing due-process procedures for all staffs and institutions of higher education. Mutual agreement on such procedures can be reached at the bargaining table—the only arena where the power of the staff and that of the administration are equalized. Once embodied in the collective-bargaining agreement, these principles will have the same effect as the law or a court decision for a particular institution or set of institutions. As the Supreme Court has said, the collective-bargaining agreement establishes a code of governance, regulating the employment relations of a particular institution.

What do we really mean when we talk about due process for college and university faculty and staff? Very briefly, due process has two parts, the substantive part and the procedural part. The procedures of due process have their origin in English common law and are meant to provide fair and equitable treatment for individuals by ensuring, as far as possible, against arbitrary, capricious, and inequitable actions. They are consistent with the rights we all enjoy, or are supposed to enjoy, under the First, Fifth, and Fourteenth Amendments to the Constitution.

Procedural due process means that there must be procedural safeguards to ensure that any adverse action can be dealt with fairly and equitably and that the affected individual has every opportunity to face his accusers, respond to the charges, and refute the charges against him. Most of you are familiar with the basic components of procedural due process: the individual has the right to a hearing; the hearing will be open or closed, at the discretion of the individual; the individual has the right to be represented; the hearing agency will render a decision based solely on the unrefuted evidence produced at the hearing; the individual will have the right to appeal, and that appeal can ultimately end in final, binding arbitration. These standards and procedures should apply to all members of the professional staff from the date of initial employment.

In America today, few institutions of higher education provide adequate due process for staff members, which will not surprise you. On the contrary, the violation of civil and professional rights is widespread. In view of the serious and long-lasting personal and professional damage done to the individuals affected by current hiring and dismissal practices, all institutions of higher education, from community colleges through graduate schools, both public and private, must be required to adopt genuine due-process safeguards.

In my opinion and in the opinion of NEA, there are three critical due-process issues facing faculty and staff. The first is the probationary period. Probation, in our view, refers to the time between the initial hiring of a staff member and the conferring of tenure, during which one's work is under evaluation to determine whether it meets known, predetermined standards of scholarship and teaching ability and warrants a tenure appointment. During this period the probationary staff member receives annual contracts of employment, renewable each year. Conferring the initial annual contract upon a probationary employee, however, carries the expectation of renewal, so long as one's work meets the predetermined standards. In any event, the probationary employee has a right not to be denied renewal of employment for arbitrary, capricious, or frivolous reasons.

A number of current inadequacies in college and university practices must be corrected, in our view, in order to provide the basis for fair and equitable treatment during the probationary period. First, the initial annual contract must include a clear description of the duties and responsibilities of the assignment and a statement of the standards and criteria of competence on which the probationary staff member's performance will be judged. Second, definite dates must be established for the renewal of annual contracts, after which the contracts are automatically renewed. Third, regular formal evaluation of the performance of the probationary staff member must be conducted on the basis of known standards and criteria, as defined in the initial contract. Fourth, the institution has an obligation, we believe, to provide every assistance to the inadequate staff member to help overcome his or her difficulties before it takes adverse action. The probationary period should be no longer than necessary to complete that process, and should not exceed three years. Any new staff member who has achieved tenure at another institution of higher education should not be required, in our view, to serve more than one year's probation at the new institution.

The second critical issue is tenure itself, which is not unlike the status of the master craftsman conferred by the craft guild of the Middle Ages. Members who demonstrated a predetermined level of technical competence in their craft gained recognition as masters. It is NEA's position that every probationary staff member should be eligible for and entitled to tenure upon reaching the prescribed level of competence. Hence the practice of establishing institutional tenure quotas must be abolished. Such artificial barriers to the achievement of tenure are unrelated to any standard of professional competence and contribute to dismissal for arbitrary, capricious, or frivolous reasons. Conferring tenure on a staff member should signify a continuing contract of employment with the institution that need not be annually renewed and can be terminated only for just cause. *Just cause* shall mean only flagrant and continuing failure to fulfill contract obligations, without legitimate reasons.

The third critical issue in due process is reduction in force, *riffing*. In the economic atmosphere which prevails in higher education, riffing has become an immediate threat to many staff people. Safeguards are needed to protect staff members, both probationary and tenured, against such action. NEA believes that we must have a position on this important issue. It is responsible to have a position—one that can be questioned and debated.

A reduction in force, in our view, should be treated as a temporary layoff, not as a termination. Procedures should be established by which any reduction in force will be accomplished; objective criteria must be established to determine who shall be riffed and in what order. All temporary staff should be riffed before tenured staff and reduction should proceed according to seniority: first the least senior staff member in terms of length of service at the institution, followed by the next least senior, and so on. Where staff members have been hired under a newly implemented minority hiring program, exceptions should be made to this procedure to guarantee the program's integrity.

Staff members who have been riffed should be guaranteed certain rights and benefits, among which the following are essential. (a) Before being riffed, the staff member should have the right to fill any vacancy for which he or she is qualified; (b) the institution should provide a retraining program to assist the staff member in filling such a vacancy; and (c) the right to recall to any position for which the individual is qualified, whether a newly created one or a vacancy, must be provided.

Recall should be by seniority: the most senior first, the next most senior next, and so on. In no case should a new staff member be hired to fill a position for which a riffed staff member is qualified. Staff members who have been riffed should suffer no loss of benefits and should be placed at the next salary step above their former step upon recall. A riffed staff member should receive from the university or college, in addition to unemployment benefits (where available), supplemental benefits from one-half to three-quarters of his or her annual salary.

Riffing is the most important issue for staff in higher education today. Probationary standards and procedures and tenure are the other really significant current issues in due process.

I would now like to discuss a few legislative areas in which NEA is involved that are of particular interest to librarians. I am not trying to "sell" NEA, but I think the connection between ALA and NEA is important. NEA's record of accomplishment on behalf of librarians at all levels of the profession is noteworthy. For many years NEA has co-operated with the American Library Association and its integral groups on the legislative front in Washington.

More specifically, NEA's activity during the past decade has centered on three areas. The first was initiated in 1964 in coordinating the work of the National Ad Hoc Committee on Copyright Law Revisions, which is largely a lobbying and media force comprised of some forty nonprofit educational organizations and institutions, including the American Library Association, the Medical Library, Association, and the National Council of Teachers of English.

The second area is repeatedly seeking to revise and update copyright legislation by introducing congressional bills, testifying before appropriate congressional committees, and otherwise lobbying and expending considerable legal, monetary, and related resources to fend off undue court restrictions on the application of the fair-use doctrine.

Finally, on the legislative front, our lobbying staff indicates that we will continue to engage in an uphill battle for achieving meaningful and sorely needed revisions in the 1909 copyright law, which is still on the books.

In a recent *Washington Newsletter*, ALA reported that appropriations for fiscal '76 and '77 and the library provisions of the House and Senate bills total over $70 million. NEA fights for those funds on Capitol Hill.

At this point I wish to reemphasize that it is NEA's position that librarians be compensated on a par with all faculty and that librarians achieve full faculty status. However, I would like to urge that you not let your historic fight for full faculty status, and all that you want as professionals, obscure what must be your first priority. That, in my view, is organizing yourselves for power. To put it another way, knowing what you want is not difficult, but knowing how to get what you want is really important. Your colleague, John Weatherford, recently wrote:

> As librarians have shared little in real faculty power, . . . they should be interested in a speculation of Coleman's, that collective bargaining will distribute the authority previously held by classroom teachers among what he calls the "subpopulation" of higher education. Realistically this may come to mean librarians as well as coaches, counsellors, graduate fellows, and students. The authority that is eventually so shared should prove quite unrecognizable as the "faculty status" for which librarians have been striving these 20 years. They may or may not like this possible new status, but they must be able to evaluate it. To do so requires shedding the romanticism that has marked their faculty-status movement.[1]

1. John Weatherford, "Participatory Something or Other through Bargaining," *Library Journal* 100:825 (1 May 1975).

In closing, I have some ideas about how you may shed your romanticism and work toward achieving the status you deserve and desire. First, I suggest that you continue to have as many conferences as possible in such delightful cities as San Francisco, with a full exchange of papers and scholarly presentations. But I say this with reservation because the problem with this approach is that it will only increase your frustration. Meetings alone will not help you do what I believe you really need to do. That is, organize for power.

If you are not "into" bargaining already, you need to create recognizable interest groups and entities on the campuses you come from. As librarians, you need to form these groups and know what you stand for, based on common interest. Next you need, as special interest groups or caucuses, to impact other faculty groups who have power on your campus: the senate, the faculty personnel committee, and so forth.

If there is no faculty collective-bargaining organization on your campus, you should organize one. Librarians can become the organizational core. If your senate is all powerful, you should infiltrate it and gain positions of leadership in it. No matter what stage of organizational development you find on your campus, as librarians who are organized as librarians, you should expand your community of interests to all faculty members through face to face dialogue and other forms of communication. Starting from your community of interest, and based on your work and your needs, you should reach out to other faculty to develop a broad base of faculty support for the interests of all the faculty. (The isolation of individual faculty members is a major problem at most institutions and regular contact and communication are essential.)

As you move into a collective-bargaining mode, librarians must secure positions on negotiating councils. You must function as members of bargaining teams, as representatives on collective-bargaining platform and contract-drafting committees, and so forth.

I would like to leave you with this picture of a group of library staff getting together, putting their house in order, getting themselves organized, expanding their interests to those of the other faculty, and following a straight line to a broad-based faculty organization through the collective-bargaining election process and all that that entails. Then picture the need to change the process. At the point of negotiating and maintaining the contract, you modify the process by sharing, as librarians, in the interest of everyone on the faculty, in every discipline or division on the campus.

A good model for what I am proposing is to be found, I believe, in the recent actions of the medical interns and residents in forcing the American Medical Association to change its view of the world and reality. These folks organized themselves and changed the AMA. Perhaps you might consider the same approach with your faculty colleagues. The place to start is on your campus.

If we, working in the arena of higher education and the NEA, can be of help, we are as close as the telephone.

Charles J. McClain, Jr.

Charles J. McClain, Jr., is associate secretary and assistant counsel of the American Association of University Professors (AAUP). In addition to his legal training, he holds a Ph.D. in modern European history from Stanford University.

It is probably well known to you that the association I represent and your affiliate body, the American Library Association, have many striking parallels and have worked in tandem on several important endeavors during the past quarter century. I note with satisfaction that the ALA was the very first organization, after the AAUP, to endorse the 1940 Statement of Principles on Academic Freedom and Tenure, stealing the march on both the Association of American Law Schools and the American Political Science Association. I notice, as well, that ALA maintains an Office for Intellectual Freedom whose functions are remarkably similar to those of AAUP's Committee A on Academic Freedom and Tenure.

Also, AAUP was privileged, along with ACRL, to be co-author of the Joint Statement on Faculty Status of College and University Librarians. The Association of American Colleges (AAC) was the third co-author of this document. I note with regret that AAC has not yet seen fit to endorse the statement; but far be it from us to abandon hope of late conversion.

Since its founding in 1915, the exclusive concern of AAUP has been higher education. Indeed, it can be said with some justification that the code of laws and regulations which govern American higher education is primarily the result of AAUP draftmanship. I refer to the numerous policy documents promulgated by the association, or by the association conjointly with other organizations, the most important of which are the 1940 statement, the 1966 Statement on Government of Colleges and Universities, and, for academic librarians, the statement referred to above on the faculty status of college and university librarians.

Academic freedom, tenure, and shared authority have become common terms in the lexicon of American academe. I think that is attributable largely to the efforts of the association over the past sixty years. We continue to perform this traditional role as a kind of American Civil Liberties Union for the teaching profession, each year processing an ever mounting number of complaints and cases in academic freedom, tenure, and academic due process.

The association has ventured in recent years into new areas. Its concern for improving the welfare of higher-education professionals has led to strong support for the proposition of collective bargaining. I quote directly from our Statement on Collective Bargaining:

> Collective bargaining, in offering a rational and equitable means of distributing resources and of providing recourse for an aggrieved individual, can buttress and complement the sound principles and practices of higher education which the American Association of University Professors has long supported.

We have determined that, where it is deemed appropriate by our local chapters, we will vigorously support collective bargaining as an additional means of realizing the goals for which the association has always stood. Since the promulgation of our statement on bargaining in 1972, we have competed in virtually every major collective-bargaining election at the four-year college level, compiling what I believe is a very impressive record. Without going into the details of the many tragedies and triumphs over the last several years or attempting any sort of post-mortem on the election results, I would say that our greatest difficulty has been not with the organizations represented by either of my two colleagues on the panel but with that mysterious competitor known as "no agent." Perhaps Professor Orr will enlighten us on why that has happened.

The program of this conference directs our attention to the implications of collective bargaining for college governance and for college and university librarians. I shall say a few words about each of these topics.

It seems to me that in exploring the implications of collective bargaining for college governance we might wish to examine the implications of college governance for collective bargaining. It is a well-known fact that at some institutions interest in collective bargaining has sprung from a growing feeling of faculty members that their role in college governance has either been seriously diminished or, indeed, has never been fully realized. At the University of Bridgeport in Connecticut, for example, the AAUP chapter moved rapidly to become the bargaining agent under a mandate from the faculty senate, which had observed a notable diminution in its power and influence over a short period of time. Even at institutions where there is a long tradition of faculty self-governance, faculty members see college administrations, boards of trustees, and—in the case of public institutions—even state legislatures threatening incursions on their prerogatives, and they look to collectively negotiated contracts as a means of holding the line against further incursions.

This concern about governance is a highly legitimate reason for entering collective bargaining. One of the cardinal principles of our association is that faculty members possess a kind of second-class citizenship unless they play a significant role in the governance of the institutions they serve. This encompasses not only the right to participate in educational policymaking—the legislative aspect of governance, if we may use that metaphor—but also the right to have a determinative voice in matters of faculty status—the judicial aspect of governance, if you will. Both of these faculty prerogatives receive explicit endorsement in the 1966 Statement on Government, which is as much a product of the administrative as the faculty community. We thus reject the view, which has been advanced from time to time, that faculty have better things to do than busy themselves with such matters and are well advised to leave the management of the institution to administrators, trusting only to negotiated agreements as a check on administrative discretion. I am happy to report that this theory of college governance has not exactly swept the country. Indeed, in visiting campuses of every type I never cease to be impressed by the great premium that higher-education faculty place on their governance prerogatives. This is as true of the community college as of the research-oriented university.

Needless to say, AAUP chapters that have engaged in collective bargaining have placed a heavy premium on securing contractual recognition of faculty governance rights. This has been done in a variety of ways. Where there is an existing, reasonably well functioning system of governance, including an equitable peer review system, the avenue most often chosen is a past practices clause, such as the one negotiated by the AAUP chapter at Adelphi University. This clause assures the continuation, as a matter of enforceable right, of existing faculty prerogatives in the area of educational policymaking. The agreement negotiated at St. John's University incorporates by reference, into the document itself, the entire 1966 Statement on Government of Colleges and Universities, making departures from its provisions subject to the contract grievance procedure. The contract also provides for the continued existence and functioning of internal bodies such as the university senate, the faculty council, and departmental personnel and budget committees.

The unusually imaginative agreement that was negotiated recently at Temple University comes close to codifying in the collective-bargaining contract the principles embodied in the 1966 statement. It provides for internal arbitration of positive faculty tenure recommendations that are not accepted by the administration and binding arbitration where a hearing committee's recommendation on a dismissal case is subsequently overruled by the administration. The Temple agreement illustrates the manner in which we prefer to see collective bargaining mesh with the traditional mechanisms of college governance. In faculty personnel matters under the Temple agreement, involving nonrenewals, dismissals, and negative promotion decisions, the faculty member is required to exhaust the internal appeals mechanism as a precondition for using the contract grievance procedure. For tenure denial and dismissal cases, arbitration is focused on instances in which the administration or governing board fails to concur in a decision of ultimate faculty authority.

Implicit in this scheme is the desire to use collective bargaining both to preserve and to improve on the existing system of peer review in personnel matters. Also implicit is a disavowal of the notion that the onset of collective bargaining must mean the replacement of the traditional system of college governance by a system of institutional management modeled after the industrial plant. We do not incline to the view that faculty bargaining agents should either cede away traditional faculty prerogatives to management, as some have advocated, or should necessarily substitute themselves for existing mechanisms of college governance which are functioning well.

The interrelationship of collective bargaining and faculty governance is directly pertinent to a discussion of the impact of bargaining for college and university librarians. Consider, for example, the Statement on Faculty Status of College and University Librarians. The whole thrust of the document is that professional academic librarians, who perform on the campus what is essentially a teaching or research function, are entitled to be recognized as members of the faculty and have the right to participate in institutional government. We have endorsed this view of the college librarian not only in the above statement but in the conduct of collective bargaining. We have pressed for the inclusion of librarians in faculty units and we have tried in our negotiated contracts to secure contractual recognition of librarians' faculty status. Our Adelphi contract, for example, makes the terms *professional librarian* and *faculty member* virtually interchangeable. Moreover, it expressly recognizes a ten-month academic work year for librarians.

Both the Rider and the Temple agreements include a comprehensive and detailed set of guidelines for the appointment, promotion, and termination of professional librarians. Built into these guidelines are a system of probation and tenure with standards of professional performance, a requirement of peer input in personnel decisions, and a grievance procedure.

The intent of these provisions is not simply to secure for librarians the award of a faculty title. I think that would be a most meaningless gesture. They are intended, rather, to ensure that along with the title go some of the perquisites of office and some of the burdens. I have the distinct impression that, notwithstanding the considerable steps that have been made through collective bargaining and, outside collective bargaining, toward the full integration of librarians into university faculties, librarians have been rather meek about exercising faculty prerogatives.

In the series of articles on collective bargaining in a recent issue of your journal [*College and Research Libraries*],[1] I was struck by the differences in librarian behavior under collective bargaining at Wayne State University, which is one of our chapters, and at Westchester State College, which is organized by the NEA. If you have read Lothar Spang's account of events at Wayne State, you will recall that librarians were among the first to become interested in collective bargaining and were very active in organizing drives among the several competing organizations. Moreover, although they represented a very small part of the bargaining unit, they were very well represented at the negotiation table and the contract that was ultimately concluded dealt rather kindly with them. For example, it gives the librarians the right to participate in the full range of university functions, which had previously been reserved for the traditional teaching faculty—including the extremely important right to participate in the decision-making process by which long-term library policy is set.

However, Mr. Spang observes that the librarians have been very reticent about using these newly recognized rights. By contrast—as was pointed out in a companion piece in the same issue of the journal—at Westchester State, where similar rights are guaranteed in the contract, the librarians have vigorously exercised the rights accruing to faculty status and have become active participants in college governance.

Why the difference? I am not entirely certain, but I would register complete agreement with the view expressed by Mr. Spang that if collective bargaining is to be successful for college librarians, they must be forthright and not meek in exercising the privileges they are able to achieve in the bargaining process. The more librarians act like college and university faculty, the more they will come to be treated as faculty, both inside and outside the walls of the academy.

Warren Kessler

Warren Kessler is president of the United Professors of California, an affiliate of the American Federation of Teachers (AFT/AFL-CIO). He is an associate professor and formerly chaired the Department of Philosophy of California State University at Fresno.

I wish to address some fundamental issues I saw emerge in the orientation literature for the conference. Do you need collective bargaining at all? Are unions appropriate for librarians? Are some bargaining agents

1. *College and Research Libraries* 36:95–142 (March 1975).

more professional than others and therefore, perhaps, more suitable for librarians? What will be the role of professional associations such as ALA after collective bargaining?

Contributing to this sort of panel was much easier five years ago, when AAUP held a very tentative position with regard to collective bargaining and NEA, while it was getting involved elsewhere, was vehemently opposing collective-bargaining legislation in California. All the other organizations, five years ago, held the view of Joseph Garbarino: that collective bargaining in higher education is a lousy idea whose time had come. Therefore it was very easy for us to differentiate our position from that of the other organizations. We were the only ones who believed in collective bargaining for higher education, and everyone else had some other approach: crying or praying, kicking their dogs, whatever.

Now that the other organizations have gotten into collective bargaining, it is very important not to generalize and not to stereotype them. I will scrupulously avoid doing that and hope that you would take the same view of AFT. We have always been on panels as the heavies—as the union toughs and goons and the ones who are strike happy. Those kinds of generalizations are no longer accurate and are not very fruitful for this kind of discussion. Librarians, I am sure, are tired of being stereotyped, and so are union people.

First, do you need collective bargaining? This depends on who you are, where you are employed, and what your work conditions are like. If you are a supervisor or senior librarian and are really treated like one, you may not need collective bargaining. I would suspect that most directors of libraries do not. Supervisory librarians may or may not need collective bargaining. This depends on the conditions, which need to be evaluated. Care must be taken to address the de facto work conditions, not just the job labels. In addition, librarians in affluent universities whose regents love the library may not need collective bargaining. However, I would submit that after those categories have been exhausted the vast majority of librarians are left, and they do need collective bargaining.

Librarians' interest in faculty status presupposes that faculty members are viewed as having better working conditions and thus that librarians, who are not treated like faculty, are often second-class citizens. This consciousness of working conditions is important as we consider the desirability of collective bargaining for librarians.

Do librarians need unions? If you are going to have collective bargaining and you are not part of management, you need a bargaining agent. And I suggest that if you are going to have a bargaining agent, you had better have a real one, as opposed to an illusory one. It is quite evident that all of the associations represented here are labor organizations, as defined under the National Labor Relations Act. They purport to be unions. They purport to do all the things that unions do. They do not call themselves unions except occasionally, but in fact they are unions.

It is useful, then, to address the question whether some unions are unprofessional, or whether some unions are more professional than others. In public employment collective bargaining, and especially in education, we have a new breed of animal, called the *professional union*. Most of the pertinent laws define a professional employee and provide at least prima facie grounds for distinguishing professional from non-professional employee bargaining units. Therefore any bargaining agent that represents professional employees is, by definition, representing a professional union. That needs to be recognized when people try to say that you can have an association but you cannot have a union, because the latter is not professional. Such statements are hogwash within the meaning of the law. If you are a professional employee and you have a bargaining agent, you thereby have a professional union. It is not a contradiction in terms.

There is a sense in which professional workers may not need unions —in a strict definition of a professional as someone who sets his or her own work conditions, standards, and fees. Lawyers are traditionally regarded as professionals in this sense. They set their own fee schedules. They review themselves. They admit each other to the bar. They disbar each other on occasion. They do not have a board of regents. They do not have elected officials who review their professional qualifications, by and large.

Most faculty and most librarians are not in that category. We are professionals but we are also something else, which most of us have not wanted to admit. We are employees, and it is a concomitant of being an employee that we have an employer.

Any time people talk about traditions of governance, they talk about shared authority, but I think we have to analyze how much authority an employer shares voluntarily with an employee. Usually the traditions of would-be self-governance and shared authority and collegiality are a facade that makes us feel better about what is a real lack of control over our own work conditions.

At this point in history, all of the major organizations are clearly attempting to be unions in a full-blooded sense. AAUP has been involved in strikes. NEA has been involved in strikes. All have filed grievances, gone to court—done everything a union tries to do. One critical difference is that we in AFT think we do it more effectively.

However, you must judge your potential union for yourself, and we can't really generalize. You may have a ferocious AAUP in your neighborhood. Your AFT may be a small group that meets in a closet somewhere and would not know collective bargaining from a hole in the wall. You probably would not join either one—but I doubt that this is the case from a national perspective.[1]

I would like to describe our organization in California because I think we have a model situation. Our organization includes librarians within our constitutional structure. They are full-fledged members with full voting rights. A librarian holds a key position on the executive board at the state level and at most local levels.

We have carried a full package of legislation to give them full faculty status in the state of California. Because that legislation has had some difficulties, we have broken it into piecemeal bills. One is intended to give librarians sabbatical rights. We have also submitted a bill to give librarians the option of an academic year at their discretion. Right now they work twelve months, but some prefer to have more time in the summer or at some other suitable time during the year. We also submitted separate legislation to give librarians an equity pay increase of 4.5 percent, which totaled approximately $800,000.

I want to summarize the AFT policies on faculty status, governance, and economic issues only briefly, because the national AFT policies are recommendations and guidelines for autonomous locals. There is no AFT policy that will be mandated and imposed upon any local branch of faculty or librarians in the nation. I would say, after reading the Standards for Faculty Status of the ACRL, that AFT would have no problem with them. AFT passed a statement supporting full faculty status for librarians at its last convention.

Positions on traditional governance are very mixed. In some areas, in some campuses and systems, the governance structure is genuinely

---

1. There are two basic reasons why AFT locals tend to be more effective than those of our rivals. First, AFT is not a newcomer to collective bargaining. Since it was chartered in 1916, AFT has supported collective bargaining for educators. It has developed considerable expertise in collective bargaining and, more importantly, it tends to attract members who want a strong union.

Second, only AFT is affiliated with the AFL-CIO. This gives AFT locals immediate entree to vast numbers of organized taxpayers as well as the support of AFL-CIO's political action network, COPE. Because the AFL-CIO is organized at the national, state, and county levels, AFT can benefit from the strength of labor, from Congress to the strike line. AFT president Albert Shanker is a member of the national AFL-CIO Executive Council. In the long run, we believe, all organizations which are behaving like unions will eventually affiliate with the AFL-CIO.

representative and librarians are included in it. In other cases that is not at all true. In the University of California system, for example, librarians are not included in the senate. In the California state university and college system, librarians are included in the senate but part-time and temporary faculty are not. We will not give carte blanche endorsement to senates that are not representative. Therefore, when people talk to us about traditions and past practices of academia, we have determined precisely where they are within the power structure, as determined by those practices.[2]

I would say in closing that I think the critical issue, if you are choosing among organizations, is not what they promise by way of substance but what they offer by way of organization and structure, power relations, and affiliations.

Librarians will have a choice. Before you appear before any employee relations board petitioning to be a separate unit, you have to decide whether you want to affiliate with some other group of employees and how far you want to push the affiliation. We believe that AFT provides the structure of federation among autonomous locals that has demonstrated its ability to give librarians a place in the sun, so that you may define what you want in collective bargaining.

I view collective bargaining as a process. It is not a panacea. It is a process and has to remain open to the input of the employees within each unit. Thus I believe that AFT has the kind of structure that allows librarians to determine their own needs and their own interest as professionals. I invite you to define what you want and to join us in your local community.

David E. Feller

David E. Feller is a professor of law at the University of California, Berkeley. Former general counsel for the United Steelworkers of America and counsel to the Industrial Union Department of the AFL-CIO, Dr. Feller served as counsel and negotiator for a number of unions between 1949 and 1967. At the university, he organized and then chaired the Berkeley Faculty Association.

Unlike those who made the previous three presentations, I have nothing to sell. I have no brand of collective-bargaining organization

---

2. Where senates are genuinely representative, AFT tends to support and reinforce their role in academic issues (e.g., degree requirements, grading policies) within the framework of a negotiated contract. Professional associations, such as ALA or the American Philosophical Association, would undoubtedly continue their professional functions and might well monitor the results of collective bargaining in their disciplines. Actual bargaining, however, would be the exclusive prerogative of elected bargaining agents.

which I will try to persuade you is the best for librarians. Nor will I tell you what our organization, or our type of organization, can do for librarians. Indeed, I confess that librarians are not even eligible for membership in our organization.

Therefore, although I think you should regard me as a resource person with some knowledge of collective bargaining, rather than as an advocate of a particular point of view, I should tell you something about my viewpoint on the problem that you are concerned with today, as well as something about the organization I helped to found and at one time headed.

The Berkeley Faculty Association was formed about three years ago. It was the first of four similar associations which are fully functioning at campuses of the University of California at this time, and two more are in the process of formation. At the moment, these associations represent the largest organization of dues-paying faculty members in the university. The raison d'être of the Berkeley Faculty Association in our belief that, in any determination of whether there should be collective bargaining for faculty at the university, the constituency to make that determination should be the members of the Academic Senate.

We have in our organization people who are strongly opposed to collective bargaining and people, like myself, who are strongly in favor of it. We are united by one feeling: the necessity to preserve what we regard as a satisfactory and, with some imperfections, desirable system of academic governance. We believe that the way to preserve it is to have an identity of constituencies between the Academic Senate, which is charged with the academic governance of the university or with sharing in that academic governance, and the constituency which selects the collective-bargaining representative.

A union, in whatever situation, is really nothing more than the aggregate of the people who constitute its membership. In my old days as counsel for the Steelworkers, I used to go to various meetings of local unions, where there were always complaints about management having done this and that. When I would point out that what they were objecting to was forbidden in the contract, the members would respond that management "keeps doing it." To that there was only one answer: No contract is a substitute for a good local union. The local union—the group of people who constitute that union—is much more important than the label you put on it, whether that label be AFT, NEA, or AAUP.

I should have indicated at the beginning that I am an AAUP member, that I am on the National Council of the AAUP, and I have been a member of Committee N of the AAUP for several years. Committee N is responsible for developing national collective-bargaining policy for the AAUP. Having qualified myself, I will say in all candor that, while I enjoyed hearing about those lovely AAUP contracts, you should also have heard of some of the dreadful ones. Some are dreadful because the local constituency of the particular AAUP chapter did not feel as strongly about academic governance issues as the national AAUP does.

The character of collective bargaining and what it will do to the academic process depend largely, I believe, on the constituency the local organization represents. It is precisely for that reason that I believe we can avoid unnecessary antagonism between the adversary and the collegial systems, between collective bargaining and academic self-governance, and between union and senate by establishing a collective-bargaining agency whose constituency is identical with that of the senate. That conviction does not speak to the question of who should be in the senate. All I am saying is that there should be an identity, so that the possibility of conflict between the senate and the collective-bargaining representative is minimized.

The question, then, is: What is the function of the collective-bargaining representative? Why do you have one, or why should you have one, if you have a senate and that senate represents the same people? Why do you need a union if the constituency represented by the senate in the governance process is the same constituency which is represented in the collective-bargaining process? The answer depends on what you mean by *collective bargaining*, particularly with respect to public institutions— in which collective bargaining in higher education has made its greatest advances.

I came to the conclusion some years ago that there is a function for collective bargaining in higher education. Whatever our particular perspectives or experiences, collective bargaining means only two things. First, it means that there is a representative, elected in a particular unit, who represents everyone in that unit if he or she is able to secure a majority vote: the principle of exclusive representation. That organization is supported by the dues of its members, and that fact distinguishes it from an academic senate, which by and large is supported and paid for by the administration. Second, collective bargaining means that the employer has an obligation to bargain with, to meet with and attempt to reach agreement with, that organization. Of equal importance, the employer has a statutory obligation not to make changes in terms and conditions of employment without first bargaining with the exclusive representative on the changes the employer proposes to make.

Collective bargaining, almost everybody seems to assume, always involves a collective-bargaining contract. Not necessarily. Let us examine the section of American industry which has been the longest organized and the best organized, the railroad industry. That industry is characterized by the absence of a contract. The railroad industry has a set of rules, developed over the years (originally by the employer), and a statute which states that there must be bargaining about changes in those rules. When one party or the other wishes to make a change in one of the rules, some of which deal with compensation, both parties meet and negotiate about the proposed change. When they agree on a change, they execute what is called a *moratorium agreement*, which says that neither party will ask for a change in that particular rule for a specific period of time. The moratorium applies only to that rule.

There is, therefore, no such thing as an overall collective-bargaining agreement, although it is perfectly clear that the railroad industry has what everyone regards as collective bargaining. I would like someone to try to formulate a similar approach for academia, because I think the railroad model may be very useful in developing collective bargaining for universities.

What is necessary, in my view, is that faculty—and I won't speak to the question of librarians because I think it has to be resolved in different ways in different institutions—have an organized voice that can speak effectively for it on decisions on faculty welfare and can represent it in those areas in such a way as not to undermine the system of academic governance in institutions where the system is satisfactory. Not undermining the system of academic governance is covered by the identity of constituencies, about which I spoke earlier. The effectiveness of representation is a function of dues.

Let me be very blunt about that. The fact is that academics are generally interested in academic activity, in teaching and in research, and they are not interested in lobbying, in organizing, or in the detailed work that is necessary for successful negotiation. They usually undertake the functions they perform in the senate as chores to be performed for only a limited time, which are to be dropped when these chores are done and other faculty members come along to take their places.

The result is that, with respect to the kinds of issues which are normally dealt with in collective bargaining, you get the most ineffective kind of representation imaginable. I served four or five years as a faculty representative on the governing board of the University of California retirement system. I have been on welfare committees, both statewide and local, which are supposed to be the agencies of the senate which concern themselves with compensation, fringe benefits, and the like. On the basis of that experience I think I can say, with competence, that the kind of representation the faculty receives on such matters, through committees of the senate, is totally inadequate.

Let me give an illustration. We have a system in California in which the state pays a fixed-dollar amount per month toward health insurance. That benefit is negotiated between the governor and the CSEA, which represents state employees generally. They work out a package of fringe benefits, and it is applied automatically to the university. Our negotiation, in effect, is done in Sacramento by another organization which has no responsibility toward the university, because its membership comes from elsewhere. The legislature automatically gives us that amount—no more, no less.

The health insurance plans, at the university and elsewhere, cost more than the basic amount provided by the state; so the individual employee has to contribute. The university determines what health packages will be offered with what carriers, negotiates with the carriers about the rates and the benefits that will be added, dropped, or changed every year, and the faculty takes what the university negotiates.

One year the welfare committee had an aggressive chairman who called us together and said: "Look, they are negotiating with our money, for our benefits; we are entitled to be consulted." We agreed and hauled in all the university brass and pounded on the table. They were not a bit fazed, and said, "Sure—whom do we consult with?" Completely taken aback, we caucused. When nobody volunteered, we selected our chairman, who did a fairly good job of consultation but whose term ended after two years. The new chairman didn't know anything about insurance and didn't care about insurance. Several years later I spoke to some people in the university administration and asked: "What happened to that consultation system?" "Well, we kept sending letters and nobody answered; so we just dropped it."

Now these are important issues; but there was no faculty input into their determination simply because there was no one with a sustained and continuing interest in representing the faculty on those issues. Right now, the university is revising its entire retirement system and integrating with Social Security. The only representation of faculty, and it has not been very effective; the only independent actuary who has looked at what has been proposed was the one employed by the Los Angeles Faculty Association. And that occurred because the LAFA and the Berkeley Faculty Association are dues-paying organizations and we have enough money to hire an independent actuary to look over the shoulder of the university actuary and examine what he has done from a faculty viewpoint. Episodic attention to important issues, which you get as a result of entrusting them to faculty members whose interests are really elsewhere, is simply not adequate. What is needed is professionalism, and professionalism requires the payment of dues.

Much has been said about bargaining units. If what I said earlier has any meaning, the constituency of the bargaining unit is of prime importance if you believe in the preservation of the kind of academic government we have at the University of California. The bargaining unit is not determined by the petitioner, as someone suggested, but by a public employment relations board, and the decisions of the PERB are in effect determined by the standards set forth in the statute establishing it. The big fight, therefore, is over what the statute says. You can have a statute like the one in Hawaii, which says that all faculty in junior colleges and the four-year campuses and the university itself are to be in one bargaining unit. Or you can have a statute which does not specify the bargaining unit but gives other indications to a PERB as to what it should be.

We have a lobbyist, paid by our association, who has been working in the California legislature to see whether we can get a formulation which will at least permit us to have the kind of collective-bargaining unit we want and which we think is essential if we are to have collective bargaining and maintain our system of governance. All of this requires an organization that is responsive to the faculty, that is paid for by the faculty, and that has sufficient resources to do the job.

University of California salaries are supposed to be set on a comparability formula, based on the salaries paid in other institutions. The university for years has "gone along" with the way that comparability determination is made. This would have produced a recommendation to the legislature this year for the magnificent salary increase of 5 percent. We hired some people, made a presentation to the Coordinating Council on Higher Education, and managed to upset that formula, which had been proposed by the council and approved by the university administration. The council, as a result of our efforts, substituted another formula which produced a recommendation of something around 11 percent. We are not going to get 11 percent; we may get 8.5. But if the university had asked for 5, you can be sure that is all we would get.

I agree with Mr. Kessler: we are academics, we are professionals. But we are also employees. We have employee interests. In the absence of a collective-bargaining representative—and I'm not peddling one variety or another—these decisions are made in the governor's office or by the legislature, not in consultation with us but with that great paternalistic university which is supposedly representing our interests.

I think that what is necessary for us, as employees, is to have a representative who can participate effectively in those decisions. That representative should be elected and have the staff and the facilities to do the job and the ability to speak effectively for the employees, not only on amounts of money but also on the way available money is to be spent.

Daniel Orr

Daniel Orr is professor of economics, University of California, San Diego, and formerly chaired the department. He has also been a member of the faculties of Princeton University, Amherst College, and the University of Chicago and has served as a consultant to private business and to the federal government.

My presentation can be understood as supportive of the position that Professor Feller has taken. Broadly stated, that position is that academic groups should seek to define their interests and their activities in a manner that is consistent with the objectives of the university, namely, the advancement, preservation, and transmission of human knowledge.

Informed by that position, I have been a bit dismayed by the kind of activity we have seen in collective bargaining and unionization on campus. I propose to document that dismay, and perhaps spread it among you, by discussing what unionization is accomplishing at large in society and the prospects that unionization can be socially beneficial in a university setting. Then I will turn to some very speculative and conjectural remarks on what you as librarians should do in defense of your self-interest as employees of an academic institution, come the time of collective bargaining on your home campus.

Let's begin with the first question: What has unionization accomplished in the United States economy? This is a question, of course, to which economists have devoted a certain amount of attention. Everyone probably realizes that unions have been responsible for moving large sums of wealth from the owners of property and highly qualified professional workers to the rank-and-file blue-collar worker. That is, since the Wagner Act—the National Labor Relations Act—was passed in 1935, we have seen an enormous increase in hourly wages relative to other components of national income.

Well, that realization, it turns out, is patently false. In fact, for as long as we have been collecting data on the distribution of income in our society, wages have remained a fairly constant percentage of total income. In American income data, back through the twenties and into the 1910–20 decade, wages have remained between 68 and 72 percent of national income. Shifts within that 4 percent range seem to be unrelated to the pace or level of unionization. So, in fact, when we passed our National Labor Relations Act in 1935 there was not a dramatic transfer of wealth or income from what we might term the propertied class to what we might term the working class.

On the other hand, economists who have studied industry-by-industry or union-by-union performance have found that unions, on the average, increase the total benefit package that accrues to such membership.

People can, in most applications, become better off by unionizing and engaging in collective bargaining.

This outcome is not a surprise to an economist, because unionization is very much like monopolization. Granting an exclusive franchise to furnish electricity puts the owner of that franchise in an advantaged position for earning income. Similarly, if we give one group a franchise for restricting entry into its activity, if we give one group the privilege of bargaining with an employer who has no choice but to bargain with that group, that group should, if it is operating in an apt fashion, be able to do pretty well. Thus we find, on the average, that unions have increased the compensation of their membership; but they have done this, keep in mind, without increasing the total compensation to workers.

It follows, then, that unions are a mechanism for bidding wages from nonunion members to union members within the working class. If we look at the way things have worked out in many industries, that indeed seems to be what has happened. Unskilled workers, those with less bargaining power, are shuffled into unemployment while the wage levels of skilled workers, the ones with more bargaining power, are increased.

In some applications, unionization has been very unsuccessful. For example, economists who have studied the hotel workers' union or the hotel industry have found that unionization has had a nugatory effect upon compensation. On the other hand, if we look at other unions we see there has been a very dramatic wage gain—if we compare actual wages to estimated wages in the absence of unionization.

In an attempt to sort out why unions work well in some applications and poorly in others, economists have looked at characteristics of industries where unionization has been successful. What they find is the following. If the demand for the goods that are produced in the industry is strong—and by strong I mean you can increase the price of the goods and not lose too much from the volume of sales—the employer can grant benefits to unionized workers and can pass along all or most of the increase to his customers. Another important consideration is whether the labor input is a large component of the total cost of producing the goods. If it is not, it makes it easier for a union to obtain a larger benefit package for its members. If, on the other hand, the labor cost of a particular good is a large part of its total cost, it is harder for the union to get benefit increases.

On both of these counts we can be pessimistic about unionization and higher education. We face a weak demand for services at the present time, a situation which is unlikely to change. And the total compensation package for faculties and university employees is an important and highly visible component of the cost of running a university.

Higher education is no longer a growth industry, to put it mildly; it is an industry which is fighting desperately to maintain a status quo. This conference is evidence of that statement.

We are all concerned about the erosion of work conditions. We are concerned about threats to academic integrity, as we put it. As a cynic might put it, we are worried that we might have to work a little bit harder in the future. We can look at demographic projections. We can see the birth rates in the mid-'50s and can forecast that we are not going to be overrun in the near future with young boys and girls who want college educations. We are worried that our salaries are not going to keep pace with inflation, as indeed they have not over the past few years, and as indeed they will not in the foreseeable future. That second concern is manifested economywide, but the first concern is in large measure specific to a university setting.

As enrollments threaten to diminish further, we are witnessing what looks to a pessimist like the death throes of the National Science Foundation. There has been a dramatic cutback in public support for research. Much of that public support had been channeled to the universities in the past and had been responsible for much of the growth in our university communities since 1955.

We face some uncomfortable realities. The industry with which we are affiliated is in for hard times; the manifestations are evident in the decline of our salary checks relative to the prices of the goods we have to buy. In addition to that kind of pressure we are under other pressures, particularly in public institutions, to justify our workloads, which by implication are uneconomically light.

Is it worth teaching a course to seven students, or wouldn't it be better to offer courses that are more popular? Is this graduate program worth preserving in light of the fact that there is a graduate program in the same subject on another campus of the university system? Questions such as these keep filtering through the administrative mechanism and down to department chairmen all the time. I think this kind of questioning will certainly increase over the next few years.

When we put dollars-and-cents figures on paper, it appears that labor unions are at their best and are most effective in an industry that is undergoing retrenchment. Let us compare two situations, one in an industry in which growth is very dramatic and rapid and another in an industry which is faced with persistent decline. For the first, consider the aerospace industry in a period like 1955 to 1960; let the railroads of 1960 to 1965 be an example of the second.

An economist who looks at those two industries in those times would find, without much doubt, that the effect of unionization on wages in the aerospace industry was negligible but very significant in the railroad

industry. The Brotherhood of Railway Workers was much more bene-
fited as a union than were the aerospace machinists because demand
was very strong for new aerospace workers, due to the industry's pattern
of growth. Companies were taking newspaper ads and pursuing other
means to hire people; wages were pushed up independent of union
activity.

On the other hand, in an industry that is being cut back, as ours is
currently, and as railroads have been for years, unions can seemingly
prevent the decline of wages from being as great as it would be in their
absence. It is possible that unionization can be very beneficial in the
short run to academics, viewed from the perspective of their self-interest.
By organizing, we may decelerate the rate of decline of salaries in
academia, but the concomitant will be a decline of nonpecuniary working conditions. We will be called upon to justify ourselves much more
explicitly.

We may not see time clocks on our office walls, but we are going to
have lots of things that remind us of time clocks.

I think that this prediction is both justifiable and in some sense deplorable. Personally, I would rather face a substantial sacrifice in salary
and avoid these other threats, which would radically transform my association with the University of California.

To the extent that collective bargaining presses hard to preserve
academics' economic benefits (and that is the major concern in union
recruitment literature), we are going to see what I can only call a vul-
garization of professional activity in universities. We will begin to feel
the mentality of the body count: How many students do you teach? We
will begin to get diploma-mill pressures: What fraction of entering students received degrees this year, and why is that fraction so low? We
will also see a lot of Neilsen rating–type activity in judging the suitability
of certain candidates for merit advancement. Student evaluations, regardless of their content or meaning, are already heavily relied on on
many campuses. I think the upsurge, the dominance of this kind of
mentality, is deplorable and inimical to the objectives of the university.

In turning to libraries and librarians, I want to say something about
a local, single-campus bargaining unit versus a larger affiliation. Professor
Feller put the case well, and I wish simply to endorse his commentary
on that issue. There is the possibility of real benefit in having a senate-
affiliated bargaining unit on university campuses. However, I want to
add a more explicit commentary on libraries and librarians in that framework. I understand that, on some campuses, librarians are senate members. I know that in the University of California this is not the case.

Where does this leave librarians as suitable members of a local bargaining unit?

Rather than give you my opinion, I shall offer some advice on how you should respond to this issue.

Should you try to align yourselves with the faculty as members of a bargaining unit or should you proceed independently with your own bargaining unit? Viewed from the standpoint of your economic self-interest, I think you should try to tie into any faculty group that organizes for collective bargaining. That piece of advice is based on my view that librarians, as a group or taken by themselves, have less bargaining power than the faculty at large.

Therefore, if you can affiliate with a faculty, you would certainly be well advised to do so. You could then—this is intended to sound realistic rather than unflattering—more or less ride on the coattails of the group that has superior bargaining power.

My ignorance of conditions in university libraries is fairly typical of faculty members throughout the academic profession. Librarians are people whom we all take for granted. They are there when we need them; they do their job. We may grouse a little when books get lost or stolen, and we wish the librarians would keep that from happening, but apart from that they are taken for granted on university campuses. In a sense, this is a tribute to how well the job is done.

Nevertheless, if mine is in fact a typical view, it does not bode well for the bargaining power of librarians, acting by themselves. Therefore affiliation with faculty groups is certainly indicated wherever possible, when and if collective bargaining reaches your own home unit.

PANEL DISCUSSION

Several broad themes emerged from the exchange among members of the panel and the audience. The following excerpts are arranged in accord with these themes: unit determination; selection of an agent and competition and cooperation among representative associations; the nature of collective bargaining, the applicability of the industrial model to higher education, and related association positions; and achievements attributed to union activity.

Unit Determination

Audience: In earlier presentations there were indications that there are considerably more local-level latitude and employee options in determining the bargaining unit than I thought to be the case. Unit determination issues with which I am familiar, particularly those that have affected academic librarians, have ultimately been resolved by some kind of agency: in the private sector, NLRB; in the public sector, an appropriate statewide agency. In at least one case the unit definition has been written into the statute. Would someone please elaborate on the latitude and options available to employees on a campus?

Kessler: The decision is always made by a public employee relations board or some such agency, but they make it in terms of criteria that are spelled out in the law. Those criteria include community of interests, comparability of work, past patterns of representation, membership in organizations, and so forth. The employees in a particular work situation can do a lot to influence the data that are put before the board.

In other words, if all the librarians were, for example, members of AFT, you could petition AFT to be in the same bargaining unit with the faculty because you could say that the history of your representation was that you were members of AFT. That is the way you could affect the decision.

Similarly, if you could get the faculty to pass a resolution indicating that, in their judgment, and whatever the law says, librarians are a vital part of the educational team, that statement would help you because it would help define the community of interest.

Audience: Mr. Feller, in your concept of a senate ideally identical in membership to the faculty bargaining unit, what role does the administration play, and, excluding the question of librarians, do all the teaching units have the same representation in the senate?

Feller: Administrators are members of the senate but they are a very, very small proportion. Deans, chancellors, vice chancellors, and indeed the president of the university are members of the senate. They are not eligible for membership in our association, however, because we have excluded people at the level of dean or higher.

The University of California senate consists of every member of the ladder faculty, that is, tenured and untenured people, assistant professors, associate professors, professors, lecturers with security of employment, and a large variety of others. Librarians are not in the senate but have a comparable organization which has developed over prior years.

I am not sure whether librarians should or should not be in the senate, and I am not going to argue that one way or the other. While we indeed may want to argue for a change in the senate mechanism, my principal position is that, whatever the senate mechanism that is charged with the academic governance responsibilities, it has to have the same constituency as that which elects the collective-bargaining agent.

It is one man–one vote; so all people in the regular ladder faculty, excluding the university extension, are members of the senate.

Audience: Does the administration have a representative on each of the senate committees?

Feller: No, senate committees are faculty committees. Administration officials may be on senate committees, but those are considered joint committees. The Senate Policy Committee on the Berkeley campus, which is the executive group, has no administration people on it. The Welfare Committee has no administration people. I do not think that the Committee on Courses has any administration people on it.

Audience: In the University of California, librarians generally fall into that group considered nonsenate academics, which is also a very large group. Would the members of the faculty association consider that nonsenate academics would share a separate community of interest and that the clerical employees would fall into a third group and the maintenance employees into another? Considering the senate as one unit, how do you see the other units?

Feller: It would seem to me entirely appropriate for the nonsenate academics to be a separate unit and select their own bargaining representative and for the clerical people to select their own representative.

There is a point that ought to be made crystal clear to those who have not had long experience in collective bargaining. The fact that you have separate units for election purposes does not mean that bargaining takes place, necessarily, without the cooperation and indeed, sometimes, jointure of several units. In industry—take General Motors as an example—each plant was initially a separate bargaining unit and elections were held plant by plant. Subsequently, those parties converted to a broader, companywide unit for bargaining purposes.

We of the Berkeley Faculty Association believe that each campus of the university should be a different unit for election purposes. We would hope that the various faculty associations, if they decide to go on the ballot to become collective-bargaining representatives (as I hope they will), will win on each of those campuses and will join together for negotiating statewide issues while remaining separate as each General Motors plant is today for negotiating plant conditions—for negotiating campus conditions and campus problems.

We think it is very important to resist a tendency toward centralization, which is unfortunate from an academic viewpoint, that will follow if you establish a centralized unitary collective-bargaining unit. The fact that we have separate units, both geographically and professionally, does not mean that we cannot negotiate common matters together.

A classic example, of course, is the building trades. Each trade, each craft, is a separate unit, but the Building Trades Council will often organize and bargain for a great many of the trades.

Kessler: I would like to make a quick comment about the University of California because we have an affiliate in that system, the AFT University Council. I think it is not open to librarians to petition to be a separate unit in massive systems such as our own. I think that unit determination criteria, such as fragmentation of units and the complexity of negotiations for management, will militate against division into too many units. I suspect that we probably will have something like one large professional unit and one nonprofessional unit. Librarians have to take that into account in deciding whether they want to push to be in a separate unit.

My hunch is that if you were to push to be a separate unit, you might not get it and might end up in a clerical unit. If you argue that your community of interest is radically different from the faculty's and the faculty argues that its traditions are so different that you do not even have a role in its senate, you might well be shoved into the nonacademic unit. That might be a problem.

Audience: Early in this program we established the principle that academic rank and status for librarians would not be an issue. Most of the presentations have assumed that point of view and have dwelt on the relationship of librarians to governance and to collective bargaining in league with the faculty. There may be difficulties with all of this identification.

In some ways the academic library is unlike the faculty. In most academic library situations, the ratio of professional librarians to other members of the library staff is on the order of one to two or one to three, and in some cases one to five. In many situations the librarians, while very interested in wages, hours, conditions of work, and fringe benefits, also bears supervisory responsibility. Furthermore, in recent years the librarian has increasingly become identified with management problems through participatory management.

It seems to me that in going into collective bargaining many librarians will have dual loyalties and consequent difficulties. Would one of the panelists like to comment on that?

Kessler: When I was in Sacramento recently, trying to hash out language for the law we hope to have in California, a good bit of attention was paid to the concept of the supervisory employee. Under collective bargaining, we are going to have to make choices and categorize ourselves. I must say that I am not as torn by that as some people are. For example, I am a philosopher by profession and I am also a teacher by profession, and I don't mind being categorized with nonphilosophers for the purpose of collective bargaining. I assume I can maintain my professional integrity as a philosopher whatever happens in collective bargaining.

You have to look not only at whether you have status in relation to other employees on your staff but whether you effectively hire, promote, fire, lay off—whether you have real authority to do these things. Now, I recommend. I make recommendations all the time; but that does not make me part of management.

Depending on your circumstances, when you analyze your real power over the exact personnel status, salary, and working conditions of associates or colleagues, it may not be as hard a choice. You may or may not be management. That depends very much on your specific work conditions.

There are some people who believe that we should have three levels in collective bargaining: managerial, supervisorial, and base unit—that supervisorial employees should also have collective-bargaining rights and that the only people who should not are management. Under such circumstances, you would still be drawing a distinction between certain supervisors and base-unit people. That needs to be thrashed out at the local level, and it is a difficult choice you have to make.

McClain: My simple answer to the question is that it is in the nature of academic employment to make decisions, to participate in decisions which, in a normal context, would be construed as managerial or supervisorial.

Faculty, it is true, have only the authority to recommend the appointment of new colleagues, the reappointment of old colleagues, and the promotion or tenuring of colleagues. However, in many institutions—as I suspect is true in the University of California—these recommendations are virtually always followed. Great deference is paid to them.

In the early days of higher-education bargaining the argument was made by administrators that these characteristics made higher-education faculty ineligible for the protection of the National Labor Relations Act. That argument has been rejected consistently by the national board in the private sector and by most state boards on the grounds that, first of all, the authority is not final, as was pointed out earlier, and that it is the nature of this kind of employment to do these sorts of things. I do not see any insuperable dilemmas that the faculty would face by continuing to function the way they have always functioned, even under a collective-bargaining regime.

Feller: I spent a long time representing workers in a plant, where the entire posture is different. A responsible and effective union takes the position that management's job is to manage; it is not the workers' job. The worker's job, and the union's job, is to grieve about management's decisions if these decisions don't conform to the standards the union has put in the contract. The worst disasters in industrial collective bargaining occur when the union forgets that this is its function and begins to assume a management role. Then it becomes responsible for the enterprise, with results that are unsatisfactory for everyone.

Management must be responsible for the results. If the plant is not making money, it is the management's fault, not the union's fault.

The union can't allow itself to be put in the position of making personnel decisions. Let management make the personnel decisions and let the union grieve if management does not abide by the seniority clause. Management decides whom to hire, management decides whom to fire; and it's the union's job to take up a grievance if management doesn't comply with the rules.

This is exactly opposite to the way we have been accustomed to dealing, at least at some institutions, with the academic process. The industrial model is not a desirable one to imitate in running a university because the faculty are ultimately the group of people who are responsible for the success and the quality of the product.

You can't tell an auto worker that he's got any responsibility whatsoever for the quality of his product. If you think that he assumes any responsibility, just think of how many defects you get in the automobile you buy and you will know that this isn't the case.

Audience: I think that librarians are much too concerned with the idea that they have supervisory responsibilities. A person could be the supervisor at one time and not the supervisor at another, just as one could be the head of an academic department at one time and not at another. Until we meet this problem of emphasis upon supervisory duties, we will never get anywhere. We need a collegial arrangement in libraries, and as we demand it, we will get it.

Selection of an Agent, Competition, and Cooperation

Audience: I have been listening and hoping that the three national organizations, besides offering good, better, and best for academic librarians, would talk about bringing academic librarians who are organized together somehow, so that they can discuss their mutual problems. The nurses and the auto workers are not as blessed as we are. They have one national organization representing them, or trying to represent them. We have three that are here. At this point you might say that there is a limit to the blessings of competition.

The problem I am raising is that academic librarians who are organized by unions are now split. How are they going to get together as union members to discuss their problems? Is it conceivable that these three organizations might initiate a conference of unionized academic librarians?

Kessler: Librarians are not alone in their difficulty of getting together to talk. That is a chronic problem of people in academia. We think we are individual enterpreneurs and that we will do all right despite what is happening to the rest of the profession.

We in AFT believe it is unfortunate that organizations have not been able to get together. We have pressed for mergers at state levels and at local levels where merger was possible. Where it is not possible, you have to choose. That is what collective-bargaining elections are all about. Now it may be that at some time in your state or in your community AFT and NEA and AAUP will finally say there are not enough significant differences among us, so we can merge.

Right now there are, or seem to be, significant differences, except in a few states. One of the chief differences is over AFL-CIO affiliation, which we consider to be a tremendous asset and strength in collective bargaining. We feel that it gives us freedom and autonomy, but some of our colleagues in other organizations oppose that and are hung up about it. However, Florida developed a merger, United Teachers of Los Angeles developed a merger. Librarians are working under mergers in SUNY, CUNY, and elsewhere in the nation; so mergers are possible.

One thing you can do is press the organizations in which you are members to stop the competition and undertake genuine good-faith merger talks. Then we can get together within that context.

Feller: The organization of faculty is very fluid now. As it proceeds, you are very likely to have exactly what is happening in the industrial scene, where you have groups of people who have common interests organized into any number of separate organizations because of the accident of organization in a particular area. Typically, in the industrial situation, they have a common employer. General Electric has about thirteen unions that represent people working in various GE plants at various places. What has developed in the last few years is an attempt at what is called *coordinated bargaining*, rather than integral merger, which has proved to be impossible.

In coordinated bargaining there are conferences at which various groups in different unions get together to work out common problems in dealing with their employer. In that case, it is a single employer. However, I do not think it is beyond possibility that when organization becomes a more widespread phenomenon, librarians can have conferences, sponsored by the individual unions or labor organizations or associations, where they can discuss and work out common problems, even though they can't work out an integral merger of the kind that Mr. Kessler is talking about. The latter is not the only solution to that problem.

Audience: The possibility of a strike arises in many collective-bargaining arrangements. The first thing faculty, librarians, and others ask is what help can you give us? When three, four, or five organizations are vying for representation of a group, it is all very well and good. However, once the decision is made, is it not possible that all these groups can get together and support that unit that is dealing with an administration that will not yield? In other words, if there is a strike possibility, cannot AAUP, AFT, NEA, and any other group decide that they cooperatively will support you?

Brown: Your decision about whom you affiliate with is made long before you are into a strike situation. That decision has to be made by faculty locally, at the point of assessing the organization with whom they affiliate. You have to explore the resources of that organization, state and national, in depth. That is when you make the decision, not at a later crisis point. It is then the responsibility of the organization with whom you are affiliated to assist you when you make your decision to strike.

Kessler: Most laws have provisions for electing exclusive bargaining agents. Dirck Brown is right in the sense that the employees make that decision when they elect an exclusive agent. However, I know of cases in which an organization was not elected exclusive agent, remained in existence, and supported the strike of the other organization. That is something, again, that has to be developed at the local level; but you are raising a nitty-gritty question: How much solidarity are you going to need when push comes to shove?

It is all well and good to talk about autonomy and to slit each other's throat in competitive collective-bargaining elections and to disseminate propaganda for years on end, until push *does* come to shove—and then, in general, we don't want that autonomy. We don't want to strike alone. We want all the money and all the muscle and all the purchasing power we can get.

That is one reason why you elect an exclusive bargaining agent. That is why we affiliated with the AFL-CIO, because we want that strength and we want the resources. AFL unions do not need to go to "independent" associations for funds when we have a strike.

Feller: There are two questions here in terms of strikes. One is financial support for people who are striking. The other, which is much more significant, is support for the strike by other employees in other bargaining units. For example, maintenance employees at the university have a lot of muscle because their services are essential—unlike what is often said about the services of some faculty people.

Now what the relationships will be between different organizations when a strike occurs depends very much on what relationships are worked out among the organizations representing different classes of employees in the given institution. Affiliation does not necessarily mean one thing or another.

I have participated in strikes, for example, where a clerical local of the Steelworkers was on strike and the production workers' local of the same union walked through the picket line. Indeed, the maintenance people and the building trades at the University of California had a strike several years ago and it was agreed by the AFT that its members were free to cross the picket line. That arrangement was made with the understanding of the building trades.

In contrast, I know of no organizations that fought each other more strongly than the IUE and the UE in the electrical industry, but before the last strike, everybody agreed that if the IUE went on strike, the UE people would also go on strike.

Working out cooperative arrangements with other sets of employees is dependent less on national affiliation than on the kind of relationships an organization develops with other organizations that deal with the same institution. That's a necessary job for any collective-bargaining representative.

Audience: At the University of Michigan we have seven unions with which we are bargaining. Now any management worth its salt is going to have no-strike agreements, as we do with all our unions. If one union is on strike, all others, by contractual arrangement, have agreed that they will not honor that strike or they will be subject to discipline or discharge. Other local leaders have to support that agreement. Whether their members have to or not is arbitral.

Feller: That depends on what kind of contract you have. You say a strike will be illegal because you have a contract that has a no-strike provision in it—that is quite correct. In California all strikes are illegal.

Audience: Strikes are also illegal in Michigan and this is causing a problem in current negotiations. If strikes are illegal, then a strike fund in public employment also is illegal in Michigan, and we cannot use our dues checkoff system to support an illegal activity. That problem is going to have to be decided in the courts.

Feller: This proves that it is impossible to generalize. Each situation is unique. But if we assume the legality of the strike, so that we don't get into the question of deciding whether something is doubly illegal or triply illegal, there is nothing written in stone that organizations have to have absolute no-strike provisions. Indeed, I can point to almost any newspaper in this country. Management will tell you the dreadful thing is that it has to deal with six different unions: they all have provisions in their contracts that they have the right to respect each other's picket lines, so that when one union goes on strike, the newspaper shuts down. Other industries, that have different unions representing different classes of employees, have no-strike provisions, sometimes with exceptions for respecting picket lines, sometimes not. These are all matters that are negotiated, and there is nothing engraved in rock that says one form or another has to exist if strikes are legal.

Brown: This business of strikes' being illegal is a principal reason why we are pressing so hard for federal collective-bargaining legislation. People in the private sector have enjoyed the right to strike, as a basic instrument, since 1935. We are tired of this discrimination against public employees in terms of what we regard to be basic rights.

McClain: I want to correct one misconception about the so-called discrimination against public employees. We must also remember that, in the private sector, higher-education faculty did not have collective-bargaining rights until 1970 or 1971, depending on which NLRB decision you want to look at. It is true that private sector employees in general had collective-bargaining rights whereas public sector employees did not, but higher-education collective bargaining is almost as new in the private sector as it is in the public sector. It was only in 1970 that the National Labor Relations Board asserted jurisdiction over private institutions, and only in 1971 was it made clear that this jurisdiction extended to faculty employees as well as other employees.

Models of Collective Bargaining in Higher Education

Audience: I would like to take an issue that Professor Mortimer touched on this morning and then passed by because it wasn't the focus of his concern. Having lived in Michigan when the first teachers' bargaining law was passed and having watched that phenomenon for a few years until I left the state, I think that there are fundamental difficulties in the conceptualization and the implementation of a collective-bargaining system or process in higher education. As Professor Mortimer said, and as I happen to believe also, we have a system which is conceptually rooted in a corporate model, and more specifically in production industries. I am greatly troubled by the attempts that seem to be taking that model, lock, stock and barrel, and forcing it on higher education—rather than attempts to modify that model to accommodate the idiosyncrasies of higher education. Would anyone wish to comment on this concern?

Feller: If anyone here is going to defend the industrial model, I suppose it would be me. Let me just say that if you remember nothing else that I have said today, remember that there is no such thing as the industrial corporate model of collective bargaining. In fact, one of the great difficulties we face as professionals is that we assume there is going to be some system that will clean up a situation we have allowed to deteriorate over a decade and that it is going to do it instantaneously. If a corporate model could do it, we would gladly accept that. But it is not going to be that simple.

A collective-bargaining law, in private industry, is a ticket of admission to sit at a bargaining table. You can be taken to the cleaners when you sit at the bargaining table, and that has happened. You sit down and exercise the right to bargain as peers. You start thinking about all the pay increases you would like, but management will be talking about pay decreases, layoffs, and the management rights clauses that it would like.

Now all such a law establishes is the right to bargain if the employees wish to bargain. From then on it is a struggle. What we must do in higher education is adapt that process to our needs. If we don't, it is our own fault.

In the so-called industrial model, every industry is molding *its* working conditions, *its* needs—period. Electricians will bargain for one set of conditions because they work in those conditions, plumbers will negotiate other kinds of work conditions, and social workers will negotiate others. That is simply the way it is and is going to be. The process is open to us, and we don't have to be bound by bad precedents.

On the other hand, we are not going to be given carte blanche and get the benefit of all the good precedents. People have died to win rights that we might think we can take for granted. We are not going to get the whole thing in whole cloth. We are going to have to knock it out in a very difficult process, and it will take quite a while, but it will not be according to a single "corporate model." Whatever it will be, it will be something else.

Brown: In my view, collective bargaining is a neutral vehicle. The process has many democratic features. All kinds of votes are taken. Faculty don't go on strike unless there is a vote. They don't ratify a contract unless there is a vote. They don't elect an exclusive agent without a vote. It is often overlooked that the machinery itself is basically neutral and very democratic.

McClain: We cannot be completely indifferent to collective bargaining as it exists and assume that once we get to the table, we will be able to mold it to our own wishes and concerns. I think a good bit more in the way of theorizing is necessary than has gone on heretofore. AAUP and, I am sure, the two other national associations represented here have tried in their own way to mold legislation in such a fashion that it speaks to higher education's peculiar needs. While it is true that every industry is different, some industries are more different than others. Higher education is a very peculiar sort of industry. It is one of the few where the employees play a very significant role in the management of the enterprise. At least they do in some institutions, and ideally they should at all.

We have generated a certain amount of verbiage on this subject, but I don't think that we have given it nearly as much thought as we should. Quite frankly, the AAUP, I believe, has not been as careful as it should have been in guiding the actions of its local affiliates. We cannot be indifferent to what our local chapters do. They bear our name, and whether or not we are a party to their agreements, what they do reflects on us. I think that higher education will suffer if we do not devote a little more time and energy to trying to shape the process more to meet our peculiar needs.

I mentioned in the course of my presentation some contracts negotiated by our bargaining affiliates which I think reflect the model of collective bargaining that we think of as the best one for higher education. There are, of course, other contracts which do not measure up to the same standard. That is due to the fact that we, as a national association which traditionally has exercised a kind of guardianship responsibility for the principles that inform this profession, have not been as assiduous as we might have been in formulating and giving wide distribution to a theory of collective bargaining in higher education which preserves the best elements of the past and improves on them with this new mechanism.

I don't think we can be quite as nonchalant about the impact of collective bargaining on higher education as some of the speakers may have indicated. I would prefer that we think a good deal more about it and devote much more energy than we have in the past to trying to shape it —from the time the legislation is introduced to the time the contracts are negotiated.

Feller: I would like to add one qualification. The character and the quality of an institution's collective bargaining will depend upon the character and quality of the people who represent the local bargaining agent who is engaging in collective bargaining.

I think we have seen that national organizations tend to have a coloration, tend to have a philosophy that rubs off on local units. Mr. Brown, for example, said that the NEA, not a local affiliate of the NEA, stands for the principle of seniority in layoffs. That is very astonishing to people who believe that when there has to be a reduction in force in the academic community, the determination of which program should be reduced and hence, necessarily, who would be riffed is preeminently an academic one.

If there happens to be less demand for French teachers and more demand for people who teach auto mechanics, the suggestion that when you have to lay somebody off you lay off the guy who is teaching auto mechanics because he is junior to the person who is teaching French seems to me an odd view, which some affiliates of NEA might not share at all.

Basically, the determinant is the local unit. I find myself more in sympathy with the views expressed here by the representative of AFT than with the representative of NEA. I think I would be more likely to identify with the NEA representative than with his predecessor in the AFT.

There is, however, a coloration that comes from the national organization. This is simply a plug for AAUP, which has a tradition of academic governance and the aims of higher education. That reputation is of assistance in recruiting people for it and in the kind of collective-bargaining program it advances, but that is just an influence. The basic determinants are the kind of people you have in the institution and the kind of people they elect to represent them in collective bargaining.

Brown: The policy of the NEA on due process and tenure is comparable to AAUP's policy of 1940. It seems to me essential that national organizations take positions on critical issues. These positions are not imposed on local units.

Orr: Going back to the question about industrial models being carried over into the academic setting, I think we can isolate certain features of the academic enterprise which have a great deal in common with almost any production of profit enterprise that you want to point to. We have customers; we are engaged in a process through time; it is a service process; we qualify to do this by a well-recognized set of conditions; we are employed by an organization which brings us together for this particular purpose; and we can identify the demand for the final good we produce, namely, education. We can make predictions about what this demand is going to do through time and we can predict what the effects of changes in that demand will be.

If one takes the optimistic view, that academic life is not really like life in a boiler factory because we have clean hands and sit around and think all the time, then we are really deluding ourselves. We can get a very good fix on the effect of collective bargaining, not only in terms of the economic benefits that redound from it but also its predicted impact on work conditions, by looking at industrial models. I know no other way to foresee what will happen, except by consulting experience and making the appropriate modifications in light of specific differences.

Achievements of Unions

Kessler: In his original presentation Professor Orr attempted to give you a picture of the impact of unions on the nation. My type of philosopher always boggles at such an attempt.

I wanted to relate that effort to something in the orientation material that tried to characterize the various national organizations. Under goals for academic faculty, it says—very succinctly, in one sentence—that AFT has been concerned primarily with improving the compensation and working conditions of teachers. That looks pretty grim and narrow: compensation and working conditions; but people who understand labor relations understand that "working conditions" includes everything: tenure, grievance rights, promotions, sabbaticals, vacations, and the like.

It is true that unionized workers have won better wages than non-union workers—about 20 to 25 percent better, especially for women—but the impact of labor unions and the labor union movement on social legislation was ignored in Professor Orr's remarks. Social Security, welfare, universal compulsory education, child labor laws, and work orders that protect people against unsafe and unhealthy working conditions are primarily the results of the organized labor movement, the AFL and CIO—not unorganized workers and not professors primarily but rank-and-file and often blue-collar workers. Much of the social legislation that has made this country as great as it is has been the product of the agitation of the labor movement.

We need to keep that in context when we talk about the priorities of the unions. Unions are not simply for bread and butter. They have demonstrated, throughout several decades, their commitment to the quality of life. That amply qualifies them to represent us in higher education.

Feller: You and I are getting closer and closer all the time. I would like to add, since comments are being made about Professor Orr's remarks, that he said something which struck me as quite pertinent. He said that he would be more interested in avoiding the time clock or whatever would monitor his daily performance than in compensation. That's a view I share. However, he assumes that somehow, if you have collective bargaining, this is going to lead to results he dislikes. I suggest that this does not follow at all.

If there are to be tradeoffs, the most important thing is for Professor

Orr and myself to have an elected representative who can make a prior judgment about those potential tradeoffs, rather than have a legislature or the administration decide what the tradeoffs are going to be. It is not necessarily true that if you have collective bargaining the tradeoff is going to be one you will not like. Indeed, an exactly opposite tradeoff might be the case. It depends upon what our elected representatives want to trade for. We have the opportunity to participate in that process through an elected representative, and that's what collective bargaining is.

Orr: I didn't mean to impugn the social responsibility of labor unions, but I will go on record now as saying that I think labor unions have consistently been devices for serving the interests of narrowly defined groups, that their overall impact on society is by no means as salubrious as has been suggested. And although it is not a point I want to argue much further, I don't agree that unions are necessarily benevolent instruments in the way they function.

My pessimism about the deterioration of working conditions comes from having looked at some contracts and having introspected on the process of bargaining. I agree with Professor Feller that if we have skilled bargainers, we can perhaps avoid the incursion of time clocks. However, put yourself in the position of the collective bargainer for the faculty of Snodgrass University. You come back and say: Okay, guys, no time clocks; we won the day. And everybody says Hip, hip, hooray for our highly skilled and deeply sympathetic and knowledgeable bargainer. And you say: But we have to take a 15 percent cut in salary.

Now, you are not going to be around long under those circumstances.

In fact, one problem is that we don't know exactly where the efficiency frontier is in higher education. We don't know how much extra workload we have to assume to gain an extra so-and-so percent in salary. If we knew these things, we would be in a very good position to bargain. We would be in a very good position to appraise how the system is working.

The choice I see is not between getting a very good bargainer who will protect what we want at just the right price and getting a bad bargainer who will do a sloppy job, because, indeed, I don't think we can tell the difference. The choice is between sort of muddling along as we have been and hoping that we are more or less protected by market forces so that our salaries don't go to zero and that our work conditions remain as desirable as, in my opinion, they have been in the past, versus codifying things like how many coffee machines you have in a department with fifteen members and how many in a department with forty-five members. That kind of thing gets built into a contract, and in my view is deplorable because it destroys a great deal of spontaneity in academic life.

Maybe we could remain spontaneous if every element of spontaneity in our lives is protected by contract. We are "entitled" not to wear ties to class because our contract says that we don't have to.

I don't really want to go to that because I don't think it's worth it.

Audience: Could I suggest that you must earn a much greater salary than I do or my faculty does? My faculty is much concerned about the pay they receive. I would think that in addressing the problems of librarians we should be aware that we often, in effect, punch a time clock. I work a thirty-five-hour week, and if you lessen my work *year*, you haven't necessarily done anything about the thirty-five hour *week*. I think that collective bargaining can address itself to those issues as well as, maybe, more noble ones of governance.

The opportunity to have a real voice on an equal basis in what happens to us in terms of our working conditions is something librarians should concern themselves with.

Audience: I want to say as a woman, and thus as a member of a minority in academic and professional life, and as a librarian, and thus in a female-type occupation and suffering all the discrimination that goes with that kind of category, that I feel very strongly that we need to address questions on power and social policy directly, as they affect us in unions and as they affect us on the road to collective bargaining.

The Current Status of Academic Librarians' Involvement in Collective Bargaining: A Survey

Jean R. Kennelly

Jean R. Kennelly has served on the faculties of the University of Washington School of Librarianship and the University of Maryland School of Library and Information Services and the College of Education (joint appointment). She has also held various administrative and professional positions in school libraries. Her principal research interests have been collective bargaining in libraries and in higher education.

Three quotations, all from the third annual conference of the National Center for the Study of Collective Bargaining in Higher Education, provide a focus for reporting the findings of a survey I undertook of that portion of the academic librarian community which is engaged in collective bargaining. The purpose of the survey was to find what academic librarians think the status of their involvement in bargaining is.

I shall relate their responses to the following assertions.

Recent empirical studies bear out the growing faculty belief that unionization means higher pay, fuller participation in campus governance and better safeguards of economic security. [Quotation 1]

There isn't anything we do in faculty collective bargaining that doesn't improve academic personnel administration. [Quotation 2]

If you want change, collective bargaining is the way to get it.[1] [Quotation 3]

The findings of the survey, which was conducted in May and June 1975, tend to confirm the first quotation. Unionization—although I do

1. "Bargaining Gains Money, Role in Governance for Faculty," *NEA Advocate* (June 1975), p. 3.

not agree with those who would equate the term *unionization* with *bargaining* in higher education—in most cases means higher pay, fuller participation in campus governance, and better safeguards of economic security.

In contrast, the descriptive data seem partially to refute the second quotation and strongly refute the third quotation. In regard to the second quotation, some respondents report that various aspects of personnel administration have changed for the worse, more than for the better, with the advent of collective bargaining.

In relation to the third quotation, the findings of the survey can be interpreted to indicate that, at least as it affects academic librarians, collective bargaining more often brings *no change* than either change for the better or change for the worse. Indeed, "no change" was the predominant response to twenty-one of twenty-four items which may be changed as a result of collective bargaining. From this, we could go so far as to suggest the inverse of the introductory quotation. If you want change, collective bargaining seems *not* to be the way for academic librarians to get it.

LIMITATIONS

Before reporting more fully the findings of the survey, which was conducted to gather current and representative information, I wish to acknowledge some limitations of the method. First, I shall describe two of the more pressing difficulties which occur whenever the questions of collective bargaining among librarians and of collective bargaining in higher education arise. When the two questions combine to become the question of collective bargaining among librarians in higher education, the difficulties become doubly serious. These pervasive and unavoidable difficulties are those of perspective and of precision. They impede both the data gathering and the data presentation because they stand in the way of effective communication. Because of the variety of perspectives from which we, as librarians, and those in the thousands of other occupations that are open to bargaining view collective bargaining, its history, its rationale, its methodology—and its terminology—asking questions and reporting answers becomes, at best, imprecise.

The difficulty of precision (or imprecision) centers on terminological confusion. Such confusion is reminiscent of a first encounter with a basic reference tool, the atlas, such as Goode's. Its small productivity and precipitation maps, with colored dots and wavy lines of only slightly different shades of pastels, suggest the diffusion which characterizes collective-bargaining terminology once it is lifted out of the industrial relations environment and set down in academic circles. Just as some children accord Goode little credibility once they observe wheat growing in a state which has no dots on the map, some of us question the credibility of a data collector who works with fluid terminology. However, as children gradually learn to live with lack of preciseness and inclusiveness— as they learn to accept productivity maps for the value they hold, that is, for providing descriptions of conditions that are typical or average as general indicators only—some of us can accept data that are offered in the same way. Such are these data, gathered to indicate the general or typical aspects of academic librarians' involvement in collective bargaining.

Although every term in the statement of our topic is colored by imprecision, *collective bargaining* may well be the most imprecise term. Eight specialized dictionaries give eight different definitions. Were this researcher to attach the tight definition of *negotiations* between management and union (limited to matters of wages, hours, and working conditions) the loose definition of *bilateral determination* of matters of mutual concern to her questions, there would be no assurance of acceptance of either term by the respondents.

In short, the data stand as general indicators, descriptions, and perceptions only. They are not precise.

A good point was made by a respondent who questioned the value of the data as general indicators.

> I find this a very difficult questionnaire to answer. The terms *better* and *worse* are value judgments, the selection of which may reflect the bias or opinion of the respondent rather than the specific changes, if any, that could be directly and exclusively accounted for by collective bargaining. I confess that I would be mistrustful of any analysis of the effect of collective bargaining on the status of academic librarians that was based on the responses to this questionnaire.

In deference to this honest comment, I wish to state that no analysis is presented here. Rather, the data are presented only as general indicators of conditions of bargaining and academic librarians' status. Findings are based on responses from academic librarians at ninety institutions, which constitute 70 percent of the four-year colleges and universities engaged in faculty bargaining. You may make your own analysis or draw your own conclusions or hypotheses from my evidence. Such hypotheses could well lead to other kinds of research that would probe deeply into various aspects of the broad phenomenon of academic librarians' involvement in collective bargaining.

With time, thoughtful discussions such as those at this conference, and the growing body of statutory and case law, bargaining terminology in the relatively new environment of higher education may become more precise. For now, the difficulties in achieving congruent perception and enough precision to facilitate meaningful communication are very much with us.

In concluding this reference to limitations in this approach, I should state my own terminology biases. I tend to attach the broadest definitions to bargaining terminology in higher education. In advocating a pluralistic approach, I am influenced by diverse authorities in higher education and in industrial relations. For example, Clark Kerr, in discussing university relations, stated: "As the university becomes tied into the world of work, the professor . . . takes on the characteristics of an entrepreneur."[2] Peter Drucker, discussing the knowledge worker, noted: "The knowledge worker must be excited. He cannot be supervised."[3]

I am also influenced to a considerable extent by Thorstein Veblen and his view of professional autonomy for the salaried as well as the independently employed professional. Veblen wrote, before many of us were born: "No scholar or scientist can become an employe in respect of his scholarly or scientific work."[4]

Finally, I am intrigued by Archie Kleingartner's distinction between level I and level II goals as potential outcomes of bargaining in the professional sector.[5] Level I goals, in his view, are immediate goals of essentially economic orientation—the usual gains sought by workers of all kinds: better wages, better hours, and better working conditions. Level II goals, on the other hand, are the longer-range goals associated with professional identification and services, goals realizable by the professional employee—the salaried professional—who engages in bargaining, but goals that are not usually sought except upon satisfactory attainment of the economically based level I goals.

I am an advocate of collegial or nonadversarial bargaining, predicated upon presumed institutional goal commonality among the various employers and employees in the academic community. Therefore I am pleased by the survey findings which indicate that bargaining, as perceived by respondents, has effected a gain in level II goals, such as professional autonomy and shared decision making.

I would also remind you, as another reference to perspective from a

2. Clark Kerr, *The Uses of the University* (Cambridge, Mass.: Harvard University Press, 1963), p. 18.

3. Peter F. Drucker, cited by Thomas R. Brooks in "Can Employees Manage Themselves?" *Dun's Review* 86:60 (November 1965).

4. Thorstein Veblen, *The Higher Learning in America: A Memorandum on the Conduct of Universities by Business Men* (New York: Hill and Wang, 1957), p. 63.

5. Archie Kleingartner, *Professionalism and Salaried Worker Organization* (Madison: University of Wisconsin Industrial Relations Research Institute, 1967).

different context, of the extremely small size of the academic librarian group within the American work force. Librarians comprise just over 1 percent of the professional work force.[6] Of this 1 percent, academic librarians constitute 17 percent.[7] Academic librarians, then, account for only 0.17 percent of the U.S. professional work force. Since it would seem that even the entire body of librarians, *if* united nationally, would not be large enough to be effective as a bargaining unit, the relationship of academic librarians to faculty bargaining units becomes significant.

THE SURVEY

Following is a brief description of the survey inquiry in terms of the problem and questions, methodology, and findings.

The Problem

The problem centers on the topic, stated in question form: What is the current status of academic librarians' involvement in collective bargaining?

The questions the inquiry addresses include: (1) What is the composition of the bargaining unit with respect to academic librarians? (2) What are the effects of bargaining on the status of academic librarians? (3) What has been the impact, if any, of bargaining on faculty status per se for academic librarians?

Methodology

Population. The population selected for this inquiry consisted of the 131 four-year colleges and universities whose faculties were reported as having chosen collective-bargaining agents in the most recently available annual summary published by the *Chronicle of Higher Education* (June 10, 1974).[8] Of the 131 institutions listed, one had closed, bringing the population to 130. Because of its relatively small size, the universe population, rather than a sample of four-year institutions, was used as the survey population. Two-year colleges were not included in the survey because the community college has so frequently followed public elementary and secondary school bargaining patterns. Typically, these librarians hold full faculty status, share faculty salary scales, have the

6. Rudolph C. Blitz, "Women in the Professions, 1870–1970," *Monthly Labor Review* 97:36 (May 1974).

7. *Bowker Annual of Library and Book Trade Information* (19th ed., New York: Bowker, 1974), p. 236.

8. "Where College Faculties Have Chosen or Rejected Collective Bargaining Agents," *Chronicle of Higher Education* 9:24 (June 10, 1974).

same faculty work year, and are included as members of the bargaining unit.

Library personnel directors were selected as addressees for the questionnaires, which were sent to each college and university. Responses indicated, however, that in many cases individuals other than personnel directors completed the questionnaires. Actual respondents included head librarians, assistant and associate librarians, other librarians, negotiators, and institutional administrators. Several institutions indicated that the responses (though they were tallied as single responses) represented reactions and perceptions of more than one respondent.

Instrument. The survey instrument was a single sheet with three groups of questions. (A copy of the survey questionnaire, modified to show the aggregated responses, is appended to this paper.) The first group of questions sought factual information related to collective bargaining on the campus and the inclusion of librarians and library administrators in bargaining units.

The second group consisted of a listing of twenty-four conditions and issues related to the status of academic librarians on the campus—conditions and issues potentially subject to change through collective bargaining. This group included four response alternatives: "Change for the better," "Change for the worse," "no change," and "comment?"

The third group of questions inquired into the impact of bargaining, if any, on faculty status per se. Six alternative responses were provided.

Identification included the name of the institution, the approximate number of librarians, and the approximate number of faculty (not including librarians) on the campus.

Response. The response was nearly 70 percent (69.22%), with ninety of the 130 colleges and universities returning the questionnaires. Responses were received from institutions with a total of 1,368 librarians and 32,729 faculty. These librarians constitute about 7 percent of the 19,500 academic librarians who make up 0.17 percent of the professional work force in this country.

Replies were received from nineteen of the twenty states which have four-year college and university bargaining. Replies also were received in proportion to the number of institutions engaged in bargaining in the nineteen states; that is, most were received from New York, Pennsylvania, New Jersey, and Massachusetts, in this order.

Findings of the Survey

Findings are presented as percentages of response to the questions, rank-order listings of related data tallies, and grouped verbatim comments.

The findings will be discussed in the order the questions were asked on the questionnaire. First, responses to faculty questions concerning bargaining on the campus and the inclusion of librarians and library administrators in the bargaining unit; next, perceptions of the effect of bargaining on the status of librarians in terms of change, if any, for better or worse; and, finally, views of the impact of bargaining on faculty status for librarians.

Bargaining on the Campus. In response to the first question, "Is it true that faculty bargaining is a fact on your campus?" all replies were yes, although three provided qualifying explanations. Two of them indicated that although a bargaining agent had been selected, in the absence of negotiations of any kind, collective bargaining, in the view of the respondents, had not yet begun. The other responded that although the institution (a financially independent medical school) was affiliated with a statewide system, none of the faculty participated in the bargaining unit. Thus 97 percent of the reporting institutions verified the fact of faculty bargaining on the campus.

Inclusion of Librarians in the Faculty Bargaining Unit. In response to the second question, "Are librarians included in the faculty bargaining unit?" 80 percent replied yes, 14 percent replied no, and 6 percent did not answer the question. The comments from those who did not respond affirmatively include the following:

> Only teaching faculty were included in the original bargaining unit. (Librarians were excluded). Librarians were later (one year) invited to join the bargaining unit by the faculty. The invitation was declined by 1 vote. The administration strongly opposes bargaining privileges for other than teaching faculty. Collective bargaining in the case of the faculty has resulted in better teaching and better administration.

> When our faculty had its vote to unionize, the choices were AAUP, AFT, or no union. The faculty voted for AAUP, whereupon the AFT, determined to achieve a foothold on campus, attempted to unionize all the professionals—non-faculty professionals—on campus who were excluded from the faculty bargaining unit. (Most professionals were excluded by both faculty and administration.) Following a bitter campaign, the professionals overwhelmingly voted *against* unionization. However, the campaign had finally alerted the administration to the potential power of a professional union, and steps were taken immediately to give all professionals on campus the various fringe benefits, etc., that they had been quietly seeking for years. They now have all faculty benefits and privileges except tenure. The university is very anxious to have the professionals not unionize, so they are about as powerful as if they had unionized.

Only one institution responded affirmatively to the third factual question, which asked if librarians were in a bargaining unit separate from the faculty bargaining unit. On approximately 20 percent of the reporting campuses, then, librarians are not represented for bargaining, although faculty are represented.

Inclusion of Library Administrators in the Faculty Bargaining Unit. In response to the fourth factual question, the replies were divided fairly evenly between yes and no. Thirty-six percent of the institutions reported that library administrators and librarians are in the same bargaining unit; 46 percent of the institutions reported that they are not. Some of the verbatim comments offered in explanation follow.

Librarians are specifically named as being in the bargaining unit although there is a question as to who is administrative and who isn't. Hearings are being held to determine this question on a college by college basis.

Department heads are included in the bargaining unit. The director, associate director, and assistant director are excluded.

All but the director of libraries are included.

Only the director of the library is a member of the bargaining unit.

The head librarians at the colleges are not in the unit and two other positions—associate librarian and assistant librarian—are currently being disputed in front of PERC—our Public Employee Relations Council. They are doing this on a case by case basis—and since these jobs involve wildly different responsibilities at the eight state colleges, it will be a real mare's nest to sort out. At the moment, the disputed titles are considered out of the unit, though the union and most librarians would like them in. Some of the people in these positions seem to want to stay out—though it is hard to say why as they will not be eligible for tenure, sabbaticals, etc. if they are outside.

Change and No Change as an Effect of Bargaining. Questions in the second section were attitudinal or opinion based. They dealt with the effects of collective bargaining on the status of academic librarians as respondents perceived these effects. Respondents were asked to indicate whether the listed items or conditions had changed for the better, for the worse, or not at all as a result of bargaining. Comments were invited.

The twenty-four items concerned relationships with library administration, campus administration, faculty, students, and the public; quality of library services and collections; budget and personnel allocations; selection of personnel, including clericals and paraprofessionals, librarians, and library administrators; participation in policy determination and decision making in general; professional autonomy; and, of course, salaries, tenure, fringe benefits, leaves, vacations, promotions, due process (defined as the right to appeal alleged unfair practices), length of workday, and number of days in the work year.

The overwhelming response in twenty-one of these twenty-four items was that collective bargaining had effected no change for librarians. In only three items did the combination of responses that cited any change, either better or worse, outnumber replies that indicated no change. These changes were in due process, salaries, and fringe benefits. The most widespread change for the better, reported by 59 percent of the respondents, was in due process. One percent indicated change for the worse in due process as a result of collective bargaining, which may come as a surprise to some, who might have predicted the most prevalent change in the economic issues of salary and fringe benefits. However, both areas were secondary, after due process. Only 52 percent reported changes for the better in salaries and 47 percent in fringe benefits.

The number of no-change responses in most cases was considerably higher than in the three reports of changes for the better. The highest number of responses in the no-change column were as follows:

	PERCENT OF RESPONDENTS REPORTING "NO CHANGE" ($N = 90$)
Relationship with students	78
Quality of library collection	78
Selection of clericals/paraprofessionals	74
Relationship with the public	71
Number of days in work year	71

The highest response rates in changes for the worse as an effect of bargaining occurred for these items:

	PERCENT OF RESPONDENTS REPORTING "CHANGE FOR THE WORSE" ($N = 90$)
Personnel allocations	11
Relationship with library administration	11
Relationship with campus administration	11

These comments may shed light on the adverse change in relationships:

Administration seems to assume a new name of management in negotiating and is classed as an adversary entity though sympathetic to the union mission.

Relationships with administration are *hostile*, some of which are due to collective bargaining. Probably would have happened even without a contract.

Since we changed administration this is a hard question to answer. I would say that things could be better if the whole collective bargaining process weren't tearing the campus apart.

Perhaps the most interesting aspect of responses is in the mix of items that received a substantial change-for-the-better response. Those six items which received a 30 percent or greater response in the change-for-the-better column can be categorized in terms of Kleingartner's level I or level II goals. Although the greatest change for the better was reported for level I goals (due process, salaries, and fringe benefits, in that order), change for the better as an effect of bargaining in level II goals was reported by 33 percent of the respondents for participation in policy determination, by 33 percent for relationship with the faculty, and by 31 percent for participation in decision making in general.

If we extract from the total list just those issues and conditions which suggest higher-level goals (Kleingartner's longer-range, professional identification, and service-oriented level II goals), the percentages of respondents who reported changes for the better rank in this order:

PERCENT OF RESPONDENTS REPORTING "CHANGE FOR THE BETTER"
IN HIGHER-LEVEL GOAL-RELATED ITEMS ($N = 90$)

Relationship with the faculty	33
Participation in policy determination	33
Participation in decision making in general	31
Professional autonomy	20
Relationship with students	16
Relationship with library administration	11
Relationship with campus administration	11
Quality of library service	10
Quality of library collection	3
Relationship with the public	3

Similarly, looking at just the true economic issues (wage and hour items) and eliminating the working condition as well as the higher-level goals issues, we tabulate these responses:

PERCENT OF RESPONDENTS REPORTING "CHANGE FOR
THE BETTER" IN WAGE AND HOUR ITEMS ($N = 90$)

Salaries	52
Fringe benefits	47
Work schedules	14
Length of workday	14
Number of days in work year	11

(Note the sizable gap, 33 percent, between wage and hour issues.)

Considering just the working condition issues (eliminating wages, hours, and higher-level_goals), we get this ranking of items, reported as changed for the better with collective bargaining:

PERCENT OF RESPONDENTS REPORTING "CHANGE FOR THE
BETTER" IN WORKING CONDITION ITEMS ($N = 90$)

Due process	59
Tenure	24
Selection of librarians	21
Leaves and vacations	18
Promotion	16
Selection of library administrators	10
Budget allocations	8
Selection of clericals and paraprofessionals	8
Personnel allocations	6

Representative Comments. Almost 10 percent of the responses to each of the twenty-four items consisted of comments, offered as qualifications of change-for-the-better, change-for-the-worse, and no-change responses or in place of such responses. The following are representative comments.

RELATIONSHIP WITH THE FACULTY

Half the librarians are opposed to collective bargaining; they anger many faculty. Half are for it and align with the faculty.

QUALITY OF SERVICE

Last year (January 1974) we finally became a staff of 3 professionals; with the new contract, however, came a quota of 35 full-time faculty; and so one of the librarians had to leave. Thus, one might point to a "reduction in quality" of service, since we are down from 3—but that was a very short-term level to use as a standard.

Because of *"faculty responsibilities"* the librarians spend less and less time at their job.

BUDGET ALLOCATIONS

The library budget has been reduced, but this probably reflects the attitudes of those who prepare and handle the budget—the library always sticks out as an "easy" place to cut—more so than any direct result of collective bargaining.

Budget allocation for books and binding is negotiated so that budget is not lower than in the highest year of the preceding five years. The purpose of this clause was to protect this budget when providing faculty salary increases.

Collective bargaining has had no effect on this area except for increased faculty input to the decision-making process. More to the point is the fiscal crisis faced by the State. Unless this is reconciled the question is likely to be inoperative, with the exception that we may discover the effectiveness of the bargaining unit should reduction in force be considered necessary by the State and administration.

Selection of Clericals and Professionals

No new librarian has been hired in 6 years. Clericals (who have a different union) have been hired; union constraints there have prevented a letting go which should probably take place.

Selection of Librarians

Selection procedures for all faculty—not just librarians—have been improved.

Policy and Decision Making

Participation has been limited because the contract is so specific; there was a lot more input (more people included) before collective bargaining.

Salaries

The union has undoubtedly resulted in higher faculty salary and lower staff salary even though staff needed increases far more than faculty.

Fringe Benefits

The present contract increased the probation time before tenure by one year in all but the highest ranks. The fringe benefits were changed for the worse in that summer courses can no longer be taken on Library time and only one three-credit course may be taken during each regular semester.

Leaves and Vacations

State-wide negotiations so far have determined that librarians are eligible to apply for sabbatical leaves on the same basis as faculty, but promotions and other issues are yet to be determined.

Final determination is still in the negotiation process. For practical purposes there has been no change here except that the new contract will recognize the librarians' right to sabbaticals.

Due Process

Previous to contract we had no due process or job security provisions at all. We now have a year's notice, but no real teeth for a grievance procedure. We are allowed a hearing before the Provost, who is responsible for the library, with witnesses, but no arbitration. The Administration says due process for librarians is "quasi-tenure."

Work Year and Work Week

Presently a court case is filed to allow librarians a 9 months' contract and full rights and privileges of faculty.

The labor review board is currently considering the status of librarians during the summer.

Attempts to gain an "academic" work year (30 days' leave now) have not yet been successful but effort continues. 25–30 hours/week schedule (35 hours now) is now being sought. All other benefits of faculty pre-existed.

Faculty Status and the Impact of Collective Bargaining. The final section yielded unexpected percentages in response to the six alternatives suggesting possible impacts of bargaining on faculty status. The response of 51 percent was that collective bargaining had *no effect* on faculty status because their status was a fact before the advent of bargaining. Only 9 percent reported that bargaining had brought about faculty status; 10 percent reported that it had been negotiated but not successfully; 6 percent had been unsuccessful in bringing it to the bargaining table; 8 percent reported that faculty privileges but not faculty status had been gained; and 3 percent reported that librarians did not favor faculty status for themselves and had exerted no pressure to make it a bargaining issue. (13 percent did not respond.)

Comments added to these response options or offered in lieu of one of the alternatives were many and varied. In fact, more comments were offered in response to this question than to any other. They verify that *faculty status* remains, indeed, a term of many connotations. A sampling of the comments follows.

Librarians had faculty status, including tenure, up to 1968. At that time the state implemented a management report from an outside agency which effectively removed librarians' faculty status. We still enjoy a *de facto* faculty status locally, including membership in the Faculty Senate, etc., which leaves tenure status somewhat up in the air. The matter is being negotiated with the state and will probably be finally resolved in the librarians' favor.

What is "faculty status"? Only one librarian has rank but all participate fully. Collective bargaining has brought about faculty status—because librarians were neither faculty nor administration before.

In 1966 librarians in this university were granted faculty status *and* rank. Collective bargaining solidified this advancement since library faculty are regarded as "non-instructional" faculty and enjoy all the benefits that classroom or "teaching" faculty enjoy, except

Work week—35 hours for librarians
Vacation—6 weeks for librarians

Librarians have always had faculty status on this campus. A few years pre-union we had equivalent rank. With the administration contract the library was recognized in writing as an academic faculty exactly equal to the school's. All librarians have academic rank (prof., assoc. prof., etc.).

The librarians here do not want *real* faculty status, with publications, tenure review, etc. We want a kind of academic status, something more than the "clerical" status we seem to hold here, more a recognition of the contribution we give to the educational process. The contract has a clause calling for a study group on this matter with a deadline for its report and recommendations, but nothing has been done so far.

Faculty rank and status was a fact *before* this (the 2nd) contract was negotiated. *Now*, librarians are no longer faculty, but are part of academic staff, with registrars, counselors, and admission officers. Also, no additional librarians will be tenured, but those currently with tenure will retain it.

During the present negotiations (our contract was out August 31 1974) the union . . . will attempt to get *longer* vacations for librarians, since we are judged by the same standards as other faculty for tenure and upward mobility. We need time to do research, to publish, etc. A 9–5 day and a 6 weeks' vacation do not leave much time for writing, etc.

The librarians in this school have never formally asked for faculty status and it is not known how receptive the bargaining unit, which is dominated by teaching faculty, would be to such a proposal.

Two of our librarians have had faculty rank for several years (librarian and assistant librarian who is the reference librarian). One of the six without rank at the time of the first contract was given rank under the first contract—the administration's interpretation. Failure to give rank to the remaining librarians is now being fought in the courts.

Although librarians in this system have the "name" of faculty, they lack the game. In other words, librarians do not have the academic year, nor do they have the same opportunities for promotion since promotions must be linked with changes in jobs. The union is currently discussing these matters with the State.

SUMMARY AND CONCLUSIONS

Overall, responses from the campuses where faculty collective bargaining is practiced indicate that most librarians are in the faculty bargaining units. Only one campus reported a bargaining unit for librarians separate from that for faculty. Library administrators are included with librarians in the bargaining units at approximately one-third of the institutions and are excluded from nearly half the units.

In response to questions about the effect of collective bargaining on the status of librarians, the predominant response is no change. In only three of twenty-four issues does "change" exceed "no change." The three areas where change has occurred, in order of percentages reporting change, are due process, salaries, and fringe benefits. With regard to faculty status and the impact of collective bargaining, over half the responses indicate that faculty status was a fact before bargaining. Almost 10 percent report that bargaining has brought faculty status to librarians.

Respondents suggest that bargaining has brought both advantages and disadvantages. Furthermore, with negotiation still in process, many outcomes of bargaining for librarians are still uncertain. As one respondent said:

> Collective bargaining on this campus has been a real *mixed* blessing!?! Some good (recognition, due process, fiscal), some bad (limits participation, faculty/administration tension, difficulty in meeting needs because of work load assignments).

A satisfied participant stated:

> Librarians here have been extremely active in collective bargaining affairs and find their position as faculty enhanced and strengthened through collective bargaining. They are well represented in all governance areas and are frequently elected as faculty at large to serve in governance positions.
>
> You might be interested to know that while we have been so well integrated into the general faculty life we are just beginning to attempt to meet the standards for faculty status and organize as an academic department.

Another, somewhat dubious, librarian reported:

> Because of the natural adversary roles that collective bargaining creates, I feel that it is bound to have a detrimental effect on the total atmosphere.

In recognition of the relatively small group that librarians constitute, one respondent stated:

> Ambivalence towards the union exists because the librarians are a small part of the union and their needs are different. A reading of the trustees' counter-proposal leaves the distinct impression that the trustees consider negotiations as a means of reducing existing benefits, and of introducing restrictive practices not presently in force. The union has yet to prove it will not negotiate away librarians' benefits if bargaining becomes tough. The librarians will be better able to evaluate the advantages and disadvantages of the union when the contract is negotiated.

In acknowledgment of union support, one person stated:

> Some under the table tactics are often tried at contract negotiation time by some administrators at the highest level to whittle down librarians. However, the union has stood by us and so far all attempts have failed.

Other particularly interesting comments include:

Many of the rights granted to us by the goodness of the President are now rights assured us by a contract.

Major operating effects of the contract lie in the huge increase in the paperwork and record keeping.

State has been engaged in collective bargaining for 2½ years—it does not have a contract yet!

Finally, as a conclusion to this look at academic librarians' involvement in collective bargaining, this profile, which, although it describes the situation at a state college, aptly summarizes the nationwide scene among academic librarians who are engaged in bargaining:

There has been no substantial change in most of the categories specified as a result of collective bargaining. Of course, there has been a certain amount of sparring and "games" playing between library faculty and library administration and between faculty and college administration, mostly to establish the guidelines to be followed by all parties in working under a collective bargaining agreement. However, marked exceptions to the pattern would be in the areas of material gain such as salaries and fringe benefits and in the area of participation in decision-making. . . .

For various reasons collective bargaining has effected much greater changes for teaching faculty than for the librarians here, but I suspect that given the increasingly questioning and even hostile public attitudes toward higher education, both on financial and philosophical grounds, we are entering an era where we will have greater need for the protection it offers.

APPENDIX

CURRENT STATUS OF ACADEMIC LIBRARIANS'
INVOLVEMENT IN COLLECTIVE BARGAINING, MAY 1975

Tally of Response Percentages

Percentage

Is it true that faculty collective bargaining is a fact on your campus?	Yes 97	No 1	Abstain 2
Are librarians included in the faculty bargaining unit(s)?	Yes 80	No 14	Abstain 6
If librarians *are not* included in the faculty bargaining unit(s), are librarians represented by other bargaining units?	Yes 1	No 21	Abstain 78
If librarians *are* represented for collective-bargaining purposes, are library administrators represented by the same bargaining unit(s)?	Yes 36	No 46	Abstain 18

With regard to the *effects of collective bargaining* on the status of academic librarians on your campus, please mark the appropriate categories below.

	Change for the better	Change for the worse	No change	Absten- tion*
Relationship with library administration	11	11	57	21
Relationship with campus administration	11	11	59	19
Relationship with the faculty	33	0	56	11
Relationship with students	16	2	78	4
Relationship with the public	3	2	71	24
Quality of library services	10	7	68	15
Quality of library collections	3	4	78	15
Budget allocations	8	9	68	15
Personnel allocations	6	11	63	20
Selection of clericals and paraprofessionals	8	2	74	16
Selection of librarians	21	4	59	16
Selection of library administrators	10	0	67	23
Participation in policy determination	33	3	44	20
Participation in decision making in general	31	4	46	19
Professional autonomy	20	4	61	15
Salaries	52	0	29	19
Tenure	24	3	51	22
Fringe benefits	47	1	34	18
Leaves and vacations	18	2	62	18
Promotion	16	7	46	31
Due process (right to appeal alleged unfair practices)	59	1	24	16
Work schedules	14	2	68	16
Length of workday	14	2	71	13
Number of days in work year	11	0	71	18

More specifically, what has been the impact of bargaining, if any, on faculty status?

8   Although faculty privileges (e.g., parking, faculty club) have been gained, faculty status has not been gained.

51   Bargaining has had no effect; faculty status was a fact before collective bargaining.

9   Collective bargaining has brought about faculty status.

10   Although the matter has been negotiated, bargaining has not yet brought faculty status.

6   Although librarians on this campus desire faculty status, they have not been effective in bringing the matter to the bargaining table.

3   Librarians on this campus do not favor faculty status for librarians; consequently there has been no pressure to make the matter a bargaining issue.

13   Abstention

*On the original questionnaire this column was used to accommodate a check mark if a comment was appended.

Issues and Strategies for Academic Librarians

Gwendolyn S. Cruzat

Gwendolyn S. Cruzat is an assistant professor in the School of Library Science at the University of Michigan. She has had considerable experience in librarianship, particularly in academic and medical libraries. The author of numerous articles and reviews, she has also served as a consultant for many different programs and institutions and has been active in the work of professional associations.

To preface my paper, I would like to state that the longer one works, studies, and observes in a field, the less one is inclined to make generalizations. Collective bargaining is no exception. What may be meaningful or pertinent in June of 1975 may be of little significance a year later. Experiences in Massachusetts may have little bearing on conditions in Nebraska. In other words, in areas where human or interpersonal relationships are involved, nothing is ever really permanent or predictable. Ideas, concepts, and beliefs, including my own, may become outdated or be superseded.

My principal purpose is to express concerns which are relevant to the welfare of the academic librarian. Some aspects may appear to be redundant in view of the earlier presentations and discussions, but are necessary in order to present a context in which the concerns of librarians may specifically be considered. My focus is on four areas: (1) enabling legislation, (2) the attitude of collective-bargaining agents, (3) the characteristics of higher-education institutions and faculty status, and (4) the treatment of librarians in the collective-bargaining agreement.

ENABLING LEGISLATION

The right to engage in collective bargaining in both the private and the public sector is granted by legislation. In the private sector, concern is with one federal statute, the National Labor Relations Act of 1935 (Wagner Act), as amended by the Labor Management Relations Act of 1947 (Taft-Hartley Act) and the Labor Management Reporting and Disclosure Act of 1959 (Landrum-Griffin Act). Under this legal framework, the National Labor Relations Board (NLRB), the implementing unit, makes decisions and issues orders on collective bargaining for both employers and unions.[1]

With the passage of the Taft-Hartley Act in 1947, collective bargaining became available to professional employees, but the NLRB, in a 1951 decision regarding Columbia University, refused to include in its jurisdiction those nonprofit, educational institutions it considered to be also involved in charitable and educational activities of a nonacademic nature. However, in what is considered a landmark case, the NLRB in 1970 reversed its earlier decision when it ruled in the case of Cornell University that *nonprofit, private, educational institutions* could be required to bargain with their employees. At that time the NLRB admitted that it was entering an "uncharted area" and would proceed on a case-by-case basis.

> We are mindful that we are entering into a hitherto uncharted area. Nevertheless, we regard the above principles as reliable guides to organization in the educational context as they have been in the industrial, and will apply them to the circumstances of the instant case.[2]

The Cornell case involved only nonacademic employees, but the NLRB asserted jurisdiction over academic employees when it established a broad unit, including faculty, counselors, librarians, and other support staff, in a decision on the C. W. Post Center, Long Island University, in 1971. In this decision department chairmen were excluded from the unit as supervisors. Also in 1971, in a later decision involving academic employees at Fordham University, the NLRB decided that although the faculty could recommend policy to the university, no faculty member had decision-making authority. It further determined that faculty are not supervisors because of their relationship to their graduate assistants,

1. *National Labor Relations Act*, U.S. Code, vol. 29, sec. 151 (1970). For a concise summation of this law in lay terminology see U.S. National Labor Relations Board, *Summary of the National Labor Relations Act* (Washington, D.C.: Government Printing Office, 1970).

2. Columbia University, 97 NLRB No. 72, 29 LRRM 1098 (1951); Cornell University, 183 NLRB No. 41, 74 LRRM 1270 (1970). For excellent discussions of all the decisions mentioned in this paper see Harry T. Edwards, "Legal Aspects of the Duty to Bargain," and Tracy H. Ferguson, "Recent NLRB Decisions," in Terrence N. Tice, ed., *Faculty Bargaining in the Seventies* (Ann Arbor, Mich.: Institute of Continuing Legal Education, 1973), p. 21–37, 39–52.

which is a teacher-student rather than an employer-employee relationship.[3]

Both the Cornell decision and the statement made by the NLRB regarding application of industrial sector collective-bargaining guidelines to higher-education institutions, as well as subsequent decisions of the NLRB, seem to indicate that the NLRB views colleges and universities as more than communities of scholars. Moreover, definitions fundamental to the NLRA (National Labor Relations Act) and to the NLRB decisions are distinctly industrial or bureaucratic in nature. For example, the NLRA defines a supervisor as:

> any individual having authority, in the interest of the employer, to hire, transfer, suspend, lay off, recall, promote, discharge, assign, reward, or discipline other employees, or responsibility to direct them, or to adjust their grievances, or effectively recommend such action, if in connection with the foregoing the exercise of such authority is not of a merely routine or clerical nature, but requires the use of independent judgment.

It also gives an extremely detailed definition of a *professional*:

> any employee engaged in work (i) predominantly intellectual and varied in character as opposed to routine mental, manual, mechanical, or physical work; (ii) involving the consistent exercise of discretion and judgment in its performance; (iii) of such a character that the output produced or the result accomplished cannot be standardized in relation to a given period of time; (iv) requiring knowledge of an advanced type in a field of science or learning customarily acquired by a prolonged course of specialized intellectual instruction and study in an institution of higher learning or hospital, as distinguished from a general academic education or from an apprenticeship or from training in the performance of routine, mental, manual, or physical processes; or any employee who (i) has completed the courses of specialized intellectual instruction and study described in clause (iv) . . . and (ii) is performing related work under the supervision of a professional person to qualify himself to become a professional employee as defined.

In addition, the NLRA forbids the placing of professional employees in a bargaining unit with nonprofessional workers unless a majority of the professionals vote for it.[4] Although these definitions emanate from the federal agency, in a number of states where collective-bargaining legislation has been enacted and the federal statute emulated these definitions have been adopted by the state government agencies.

3. Long Island University (C. W. Post), 189 NLRB No. 109, 77 **LRRM** 1001 (1971); Fordham University, 193 NLRB No. 23, 78 LRRM 1177 (1971).

4. William P. Lemmer has pulled together pertinent definitions set forth by either NLRA or NLRB decisions in "The Bargaining Unit," in Tice, *Faculty Bargaining*, p. 54–57.

The emulation of federal legislation and the adoption of federal agency definitions is common practice in states with collective-bargaining legislation because no attempt has been made to establish uniform law or to propose a model law. Consequently, states and municipalities vary in the comprehensiveness of the legislation. In addition, administrative law, in the form of President Kennedy's Executive Order 10988 of 1962 and President Nixon's Executive Order 11491 of 1969, has provided a basis for collective bargaining among local, state, and federal agency employees.[5]

Collective bargaining in the public sector, then, does not have the clear-cut authority it has in the private sector. Therefore public higher-education institutions, in contrast with private higher-education institutions, are able to bargain only if their state provides coverage, which is usually more restrictive than that provided by federal legislation. Further, even when the state government has adopted the legislation and the definitions of the federal government regarding collective bargaining, there is no guarantee that the interpretation of these statutes and definitions will be the same for the private and public sectors.

Both federal and state collective-bargaining legislation identifies bargaining unit determination as the first step in the collective-bargaining process, whether by the mutual consent of those seeking recognition as a unit or by federal or state agency decision. Unit determination is perhaps the most significant step as well, because in addition to establishing the persons who are represented it has a decided impact on the shape of negotiations.

In determination of an appropriate bargaining unit, what happens to academic librarians? How do the previously mentioned definitions apply? Do they apply in the library environment? If so, how, and to whom?

Thus far the membership of collective-bargaining units in higher-education institutions has been determined on a case-by-case basis, usually through a combination of conditions or attitudes at an institution and the federal or state agency's application or interpretation of the law in that specific situation. Consequently, the group of employees engaging in collective bargaining in a higher-education institution, while often termed *faculty*, is generally a much broader group than what is traditionally known as faculty. At present, almost all collective-bargaining agreements include librarians with full-time faculty in the bargaining units. While a number of these faculties have voluntarily admitted academic librarians to their ranks, with full voting power, there has been notable evidence that most librarians have been included in the bargain-

5. U.S. President, Executive Order, "Labor-Management Relations in the Federal Service," *Federal Register*, vol. 34 (October 29 1969).

ing units through determination of the unit by the governmental agency. The significant point is that the governmental unit has not made a distinction between faculty and staff or between academic and nonacademic personnel, nor has the agency attempted to define these terms. A clear example is in the state of Hawaii, where the governmental unit has designated the faculty of the University of Hawaii and the community college system as the appropriate bargaining unit, but has not defined *faculty*.

Seemingly, there is a predilection among state government agencies for the broad unit. For example, the Michigan Employment Relations Committee (MERC) prescribes that the appropriate unit should always be "the largest unit which in the circumstances of the particular case is most compatible with the effectuation of the purposes" of the state statute. In the case involving Wayne State University, MERC determined that all nonsupervisory employees of the university who are involved in educating and developing students—the graduate and undergraduate faculty, the faculties of professional schools (including law and medicine), counselors, librarians, and residence hall advisors—should be included in a single unit. Noting the broad community of interest among them, it emphasized avoidance of fragmentation of bargaining units.

Wayne's administration had sought separate bargaining units for faculty and administrative staff, which included librarians, and separate representation for the medical school faculty.[6] MERC's view differed sharply from that in the NLRB decision in the Fordham case. The NLRB specifically excluded the law faculty from the general faculty unit because of differences in professional interest, location, and pay scales (among others). These differences illustrate that interpretations of what is basically the same statute can vary in the private and public sectors.

In another landmark case, which has particular import for academic librarians, the NLRB determined (regarding Claremont University Center) that the full-time and regular part-time professional and nonprofessional employees of the Honnold Library System constituted an identifiable group of employees with a separate community of interest.[7] Claremont's administration had contended that all nonacademic employees from all colleges in the system should have been included in the unit. The NLRB, in making the decision, differentiated between the Claremont case and that of Cornell, where a separate claim by library personnel was turned down, because at Claremont the petitioning union wanted an election among library employees only. One may conclude

6. Edwards, "Legal Aspects," p. 25.
7. Claremont University Center, 198 NLRB No. 121, 81 LRRM 1317 (1972).

from this decision that academic librarians and the supportive personnel of a library system that is not a part of any of the colleges it serves may organize themselves separately in an appropriate unit. Again, interpretation of basically the same statute has been different for private colleges and universities from the interpretation for public institutions.

As previously stated, state government agencies seem to favor the broad unit. The NLRB, while also inclined to include all of an institution's professional employees in a unit, at the same time makes an effort to ensure satisfaction of the law's definition of *professional* before doing so. In the Post case, for example, it justified inclusion of librarians in the faculty unit by noting that each librarian had a master's degree in library science. For the academic librarian involved in bargaining unit determination, it is important from the outset to know what definitions are applicable.

The definition of professional may permit the exclusion of a group simply on the basis that *all* the requirements for professional designation are not met. If state agencies were to apply this interpretation in making their decisions about the appropriate bargaining unit, a different pattern might emerge. Some librarians might be termed *nonprofessional*, as evidenced by a recent decision under Executive Order 11491, as amended. The assistant secretary of labor for Labor-Management Relations, under whose jurisdiction determination of appropriate bargaining units for federal employees falls, decided in a case involving the U.S. Army Safeguard Logistics Command and the U.S. Army Safeguard Systems Command in Huntsville, Alabama, that the librarian is not a professional employee. His decision was based on the almost identical definition of professional used by the NLRB. Apparently there was no challenge to this decision.[8]

The inclusion of academic librarians in faculty collective-bargaining units appears to be the rule more than the exception. However, the variance of decisions regarding appropriate bargaining units in the public, private, and federal sectors, while based on a common denominator, implies that academic librarians cannot take this inclusion for granted.

If they are included in the bargaining unit, academic librarians, recognizing that majority rule prevails, must (1) achieve high visibility in the unit, (2) secure key positions in the unit, (3) maintain an informal alliance with both faculty and professionals in the unit, and (4) *repeatedly demand* that the bargaining agent be sensitive to their needs. Except for the last point, this course of action is applicable to all academic

---

8. U.S. Department of Labor, *Decisions and Reports on Rulings of Assistant Secretary of Labor for Labor-Management Relations Pursuant to Executive Order 11491*, vol. 2, Jan. 1–Dec. 31, 1972, A/SLMR No. 224.

librarians, whether or not they are involved in collective bargaining. If or when bargaining comes to the campus, they are in positions of influence rather than vulnerability.

Enabling state legislation, however, does not always guarantee funding in support of negotiated settlements. As indicated in earlier presentations, lobbying at the legislative level, as is being done for the California systems, can be very effective. Academic librarians can lobby successfully, as is demonstrated by the efforts of University of Wisconsin librarians in retention of faculty status.[9]

ATTITUDE OF COLLECTIVE-BARGAINING AGENTS

The second area to which academic librarians should give attention is organizations which wish to represent faculty in higher-education institutions. To give historical or general descriptions of these organizations would be unduly redundant, but the American Association of University Professors (AAUP), the American Federation of Teachers (AFT), and the National Education Association (NEA) are competing vigorously for the right to represent faculty in collective bargaining. What has been their attitude toward librarians?

The AAUP, traditionally concerned with the professoriate, discovered that the state and federal agencies were including groups in the bargaining unit that were excluded from its membership. The legislative requirements and political implications, among other factors, caused AAUP to amend its constitution in 1972 so as to admit other groups, including librarians. Previously, only librarians with faculty status were eligible. Both AFT and NEA had bases in the public schools; consequently, they represent a large majority of community college faculties. Each has become the agent for a number of four-year institutions, but their biggest success has been their merged affiliates in the state of New York.

When it has been necessary to define the appropriate bargaining unit, AAUP has usually tried to limit the membership to faculty. AFT and NEA have vacillated. At Wayne State University the NEA supported AAUP's faculty-only unit, while AFT wanted separate units. At CUNY, in contrast, AFT wanted all groups included. In addition, all have taken different positions in different situations on whether there should be separate elections and bargaining representatives for each campus of a college or university system.

9. "Faculty Status at Issue in Wisconsin Assembly," *American Libraries* 4:592–93 (November 1973) and "Wisconsin Librarians Win Faculty Status Victory," *Library Journal* 100:440 (March 1, 1975).

Academic librarians must keep in mind that, regardless of nationally declared or locally espoused doctrines and specifically stated professional or economic goals, all three associations are extremely opportunistic and political, tending to back the group or groups through which they think they can win local elections. While all three profess to support the concept of faculty status for librarians, they defer to local autonomy when it comes to accountability. Again, it is necessary to make sure that the bargaining agent not only is sensitive to the needs of the academic librarian but responsive as well—in actions, not lip service. Lack of skill in negotiating is and has been a characteristic of collective bargaining in higher education.

CHARACTERISTICS OF HIGHER-EDUCATION INSTITUTIONS AND FACULTY STATUS

The third area of significance to academic librarians is the nature of higher-education institutions that engage in collective bargaining. Librarians must be aware of the type of environment in which collective bargaining has emerged.

Collective bargaining in higher education has had its greatest success among community colleges. In addition to their historic ties to the public school system, other suggested reasons for collective bargaining's progress in two-year college environments have been (1) faculty unrest and the desire for higher wages, with expressed dissatisfaction that salaries and working conditions, heavy teaching loads, long hours, and few fringe benefits were similar to those in secondary, rather than higher, education; (2) faculty perception of a lack of desirable roles in institutional government, with unilateral decisions by trustees and administrators and faculty participation either weak or lacking; and (3) underdeveloped or nonexistent concepts of professionalism, with emphasis primarily on teaching rather than on scholarship and research and with faculty looking more to secondary than to higher education.[10]

Collective bargaining is practiced in both private and public four-year colleges and universities. Factors contributing to involvement of these institutions in the process have been (1) the widely discussed financial crises of senior higher-education institutions, caused in part by expanded enrollments and lack of support from private, state, and fed-

10. Ronald C. Brown, "Professors and Unions: The Faculty Senate: An Effective Alternative to Collective Bargaining in Higher Education?" *William and Mary Law Review* 12:257–59 (Winter 1970). George W. Angell, "Two-Year College Experience," in E. D. Duryea, Robert S. Fiske, and associates, *Faculty Unions and Collective Bargaining* (San Francisco: Jossey-Bass, 1973), p. 87–107.

eral sources and resulting in severe cutbacks in monies available for salaries, services, and facilities; (2) the scrutiny of governance mechanisms, especially those relating to economic status, at these institutions; and (3) as mentioned previously, the changing attitudes of federal, state, and local governments toward collective-bargaining rights for public employees and NLRB's decision to redetermine its jurisdiction with regard to private colleges and universities. The combination of these factors seems to have resulted in a more positive attitude toward collective bargaining by the faculties of these senior higher-education institutions.

In terms of both types of higher-education institutions, the record of collective bargaining can be categorized as community college level and four-year state and municipal college level. Except for the multicampus institutions such as SUNY and CUNY, and possibly Rutgers and the University of Hawaii, no major or high-level research-oriented university, or what Lipset in a recent issue of *Change* refers to as the "star system" of American academe, has turned to collective bargaining. There is a possibility that, voting independently, the larger campus units of SUNY and CUNY might have rejected it. Even AAUP's successes have been in the middle tier of academe.[11]

Garbarino states that the most important force at work is the new or emerging four-year institution. The changing of teachers' colleges into state universities has provided the most favorable climate for collective bargaining. Systems of higher education, undergoing many changes in the last two decades, have created dilemmas that foster collective bargaining.

Another strong factor has been the enabling legislation in states such as New York, New Jersey, Massachusetts, Michigan, Pennsylvania, and Nebraska, plus the labor and industrial characteristics of the states.[12]

An equally strong factor has been the composition of the faculty and their professional self-image at these institutions. When the institution's mission changed and its educational functions broadened, faculty could no longer accept the relatively limited role they played in decision making. They expected professional independence and influence in policy making. When their expectations were not met, collective bargaining seemed a viable alternative. Two national surveys of major significance, one supported by the Carnegie Commission on Higher Education in 1969 and the other by the American Enterprise Institute for Public

11. Seymour M. Lipset, "Faculty Unions and Collegiality," *Change* 7:40 (March 1975).

12. Joseph W. Garbarino, "Emergence of Collective Bargaining," in Duryea, *Faculty Unions*, p. 4.

Policy Research in 1972, further describe the climate in which collective bargaining gains recognition in higher education.

In the 1969 Carnegie survey, which included two-year colleges, 59 percent of all faculty members endorsed collective bargaining in principle by rejecting the statement that "collective bargaining by faculty members has no place in a college or university." Forty-seven percent of the faculty agreed that "there are circumstances in which a strike would be a legitimate means of collective action for faculty members." In the 1972 survey, which did not include two-year colleges, the faculty members were almost evenly divided in their views of the progress of unionization since the 1969 survey. Forty-four percent did not agree "that the recent growth of unionization of college and university faculty is beneficial and should be extended," while 43 percent agreed. Although Ladd and Lipset did not think a trend could be ascertained from these responses, they concluded that much abstract support was present for collective bargaining in 1969 and that in 1972, after a three-year interval during which unionization made progress, faculty members were evenly divided about its benefits.[13]

A more important part of both surveys was the examination of the characteristics of faculty who are supportive of unionization and collective bargaining. The Carnegie survey data revealed faculty support for unionization to be lowest at the elite universities or high-status centers of higher education and highest at the two-year colleges. Data on the status of individual faculty indicated that the professor of low scholarly achievement, the untenured professor, and the low-salaried professor were more supportive than their more productive and better-rewarded associates. Interestingly, the 1972 survey also suggested that faculty involved primarily in teaching at the less prestigious institutions were decidedly more conservative in their political views, or less receptive to the unionization concept, than their elitist university counterparts. The faculty, usually of high scholarly achievement, at the elitist or major research institutions also presented a paradox. According to the survey, their liberalism should have caused them to support collective bargaining, but their academic values prevented them from doing so.[14]

In commentary on the reliability of their survey data, Ladd and Lipset cited supportive data from a 1973 study by Aussieker and Garbarino in which the relationship between academic quality and a collective bargaining agent was analyzed:

13. Everett C. Ladd, Jr., and Seymour M. Lipset, *Professors, Unions, and American Higher Education* (Berkeley, Calif.: Carnegie Commission on Higher Education, 1973), p. 11.

14. Ibid., p. 16–17.

They report that two-thirds of faculty who have selected bargaining representatives "are to be found in schools of the low category" or in two-year community colleges. No high-quality universities are currently represented and most of the unionized staff classified as at "medium quality" schools are in the extremely heterogeneous and multicampus New York public universities.[15]

Academic librarians may recognize their own institutions and faculty among those described. The characteristics should enable them better to understand organization to advance collective interests, efforts to retain the status quo, or organization to resist any attempt at unionization.

How does faculty status for librarians relate to this discussion of characteristics of higher-education institutions and collective bargaining? The first point to be considered is the relationship between the characteristics of higher-education institutions and faculty status. Ironically, the move for faculty status began to gain momentum in the early 1960s and emerged full fledged in 1969, covering the same time span that saw the academic culture of the 1960s, characterized by the professionalization of higher education, the rising status of the professoriate, and the trend of shared authority among faculty and administration. Also occurring at this time was the change in government's attitude toward the rights of public employees at the federal, state, and local levels.

While the statement can be made that academic librarians in general favor faculty status, as evidenced by the approval of the Joint Statement on Faculty Status of College and University Librarians by the Association of College and Research Libraries (ACRL) of the American Library Association (ALA), there is no guarantee that faculty status will be granted to librarians at all higher-education institutions. A primary reason is that some members of the academic community do not perceive the librarian as faculty.

Traditionally, the terms *faculty* and *professoriate* have been equated with university teaching. The professoriate in American colleges and universities has established an elaborate reward system, including methods of achievement and status, about which it feels strongly. It may be true that the community-of-scholars image may have eroded or become blurred for some; nevertheless, schools and departments zealously guard their power and young or nontenured professors seek ways to achieve tenure, indicating that in spite of much rhetoric the reward system is still in operation. Educators and sociologists have long observed that the ranking of faculty into full professors, associate professors, assistant professors, and instructors does not affect collegiality as long as members of the lower ranks desire higher status and are willing to adhere to the

15. Ibid., p. 18.

requirements necessary to achieve that status. These feelings have evolved from the traditions of academia, supported by the tenure system, and from independence values derived from professionalism concepts. Sanford Kadish, former AAUP president, put it thus:

> Professionalism represents a particular set of beliefs, ideals, and convictions concerning the conditions under which one's work is, or should be, performed. This set of ideas centers principally upon three conceptions—that of specialized expertise, of autonomy, and of service.
> . . . Turning to the university professor as professional, it will be observed that the community of scholars' image suggests the special attributes of his role. . . . Along with the law, the clergy, and medicine, his is one of the oldest of the professions, with its roots in the middle ages.[16]

Interestingly enough, AAUP, which represents the professoriate, gave its support to the Joint Statement on Faculty Status of College and University Librarians; but this action may not have been as spontaneous as it appeared. In an effort to maintain its influence in the academic community, AAUP officially entered the collective-bargaining arena in 1972 and at the same time expanded its membership base to include not only teachers and research scholars but librarians, counselors with faculty status, and any professional appointee included in a collective representation unit with the faculty. Previously, librarians were considered for membership only if they had been officially accorded faculty status at their institution.

Both of these actions involved lengthy deliberations by AAUP. One must remember also that there had been a steady decline in AAUP membership during the seventies. Consequently, support for the joint statement was aided, no doubt, by the combination of these factors: declining membership and pressure by other bargaining agents competing for the higher-education market. Approval by 394 AAUP delegates, while significant, should not be misconstrued as support or approval from the total AAUP membership, which numbered 85,624, or from the academic community as a whole.[17]

The Association of American Colleges (AAC), comprised of administrative representatives from member instiutions, has not yet approved

16. Sanford H. Kadish, "The Strike and the Professoriate," *AAUP Bulletin* 54:161–62. (Summer 1968).

17. In 1973, 18,181—or 21 percent—of the 1972 membership did not renew. The net change in membership between January 1, 1973 (85,624), and January 1, 1974 (75,069), was a drop of 10,555, and the largest decline in AAUP history. For membership figures and deliberations see reports of AAUP Council and Committee F in *AAUP Bulletin*, 1971–74. A description of those who are eligible for membership can be found in every *AAUP Bulletin*. For a report of the 59th annual meeting see the June 1973 issue of the *AAUP Bulletin*.

the joint statement. Reportedly there is antipathy among AAC members toward extending academic benefits, especially tenure, to librarians.[18]

Simply stated, librarians in general have approved of and support faculty status; but faculty status for librarians, even with AAUP delegates' approval, is not a fait accompli at all higher-education institutions.

The second point to be considered is that collective bargaining has been regarded by some librarians as a vehicle for achieving parity in the academic community. Inclusion of librarians in the collective-bargaining unit has the appearance of bringing about the collegiality that the idea of a community of scholars suggests, but two factors run counter to this ideal. First, collective-bargaining legislation supports the premise that the interests of the collective unit are paramount. That is, individual or specific group needs of the unit must be evaluated in terms of the collective interest, which is often interpreted as that of the majority of the membership. In the collective-bargaining units, which include both librarians and traditional faculty, traditional faculty are in the majority.

Second, the professoriate or faculty has usually interpreted collegiality narrowly, to apply to its own members. Evidence that librarians are not included in this group is prevalent in writings about trends and issues in higher education. Observers of the collective-bargaining scene, when writing about librarians and other campus groups, such as counselors, student personnel officers, and the like, have labeled them nonteaching professionals, nonteaching professional support staff, or simply support staff (the abbreviation NTP is already much in use).

Discussing collective bargaining in environments such as the University of California, Berkeley, or the University of Wisconsin, Madison, Ladd and Lipset make the following observation:

> There can be little doubt that at such schools the majority of academics do not see the need for formal collective bargaining representation, given the power of their faculty self-government institutions. But some of them face the prospect, as with the Hawaii main campus faculty that their desires may be frustrated by inclusion in a collective bargaining unit with faculty at less prestigious parts of the state system, or with the numerous NTPs. "Non-ladder" lecturers, librarians, research and extension "specialists," and the like, typically give more support to unionism than does the faculty; they have lower incomes and status and are largely unrepresented in professorial self-government organs.[19]

In summary, the academic librarian must recognize the following: (1) higher-education institutions may have certain characteristics that

18. "Annual Report of the President, 1972–73," *College and Research Libraries News* 34:196 (July/August 1973).

19. Ladd, *Professors, Unions*, p. 57.

will either foster or frustrate collective bargaining; (2) while faculty status has been approved by most academic librarians, the narrowness with which traditional faculty view collegiality tends to limit the achievement of faculty status for librarians at higher-education institutions; (3) while librarians have been included generally in the collective-bargaining unit, inclusion has not brought about full "faculty status" or parity; and (4) collective bargaining so far has not proved itself to be a reliable vehicle for achieving either faculty status or total parity for librarians. Emphasis has been placed on the relationship of faculty status to collective bargaining because many librarians have seen collective bargaining as a means of gaining higher status in the academic community.

I cannot close without mentioning that some librarians in higher-education institutions are concerned with neither collective bargaining nor faculty status. Academic librarians in the so-called elitist universities or in those universities striving for status may not see in the present or immediate future any movement toward collective bargaining on their campuses. Much of the concern in these environments is for damage to professional status, restriction or loss of academic freedom, to which tenure is inextricably tied, and the fear of use of the strike weapon in the academic environment. The academic librarians in such environments have been accorded, in most instances, status as librarians. That is, they play a role in the governance of many of these institutions by having representation in the institutions' senates or other policy making bodies. They also serve on the standing and special committees appointed by these bodies. There are also institutions, such as Harvard University, where librarians decided to work for a kind of status different from that of the faculty.

TREATMENT OF ACADEMIC LIBRARIANS
IN THE BARGAINING AGREEMENT

The experience of academic librarians in collective bargaining is still quite limited, so that any identification of gains or losses as trends can be only speculative.

The definition of *bargaining unit* for some institutions has meant broad, all-inclusive groups, such as those at SUNY, CUNY, or Rutgers. Other definitions have been more narrow, concerned only with regular faculty, librarians, and research personnel. Some have made no distinctions, except for initial statements that have applicability for all members of the unit.

Areas in which academic librarians appear to be treated no differently than others who are covered by the contract are grievance procedures, sick leave and other leaves (such as maternity), jury duty, etc., and fringe benefits. Almost all contracts have clauses dealing with management rights and bargaining agents, retrenchment or reduction in staff, personnel files, and no-strike and no-lockout clauses, as well as statements on academic freedom and nondiscriminatory clauses. Retrenchment clauses are largely based on seniority; however, some allow voluntary cutbacks by departments.

Areas in which there appear to be differences are those in which the traditional faculty has the most concern: reappointment, tenure, and promotions. In most instances elaborate mechanisms have been established to grant these "rewards" to "deserving" faculty. Almost all have had a campuswide committee that makes recommendations to the president of the institution. The mechanism that is open to librarians, then, is usually scrutiny of their work by this campuswide committee. In some instances a librarians' committee can go directly to the president and to a special committee on tenure or its counterpart.

Many agreements spell out the criteria for promotion and almost all use the standard classification of professor, associate professor, assistant professor, and instructor and indicate requirements for each level. The criteria include items such as teaching effectiveness, fulfillment of professional responsibility, mastery of subject matter, contributions to the college and community, and continuing scholarly growth. While some agreements substitute professional effectiveness for teaching effectiveness, the rest of the criteria for promotion are the same for librarians as for traditional faculty.

Although peer evaluation remains central in promotion, evaluation procedures vary for librarians. Faculty, again, are evaluated by an elaborate system, usually in two or three tiers, including observation in the performance of duties and student evaluations. Librarians usually are evaluated by one unit, the library, and recommendations are made directly to the president of the institution or to a special subcommittee for librarians.

Workload is described in extreme detail for teaching faculty in most contracts; however, a description of the five-day week or thirty-five-hour week is typical for librarians. In addition, vacation time is defined and, in some contracts, confined to a specific time span. A number of contracts even specify library hours and book budget. In a few contracts, detailed listings of the librarian's responsibilities are given. Merit increases are generally included and their allocation is left to the discretion of the administration.

Indications are that salary improvements have been made through collective bargaining. However, in a number of contracts the scale for librarians is not equitable in relation to that for faculty. In many institutions where faculty status was established prior to collective bargaining, there appears to be no direct distinction in terms of salary, but there may be several variables. In many instances librarians are on a twelve-month year, rather than on the academic year. Interesting innovations, such as formulas for the weighting of departments, may play a role in salary determination, and are not negotiable or grievable. Another variation in the salary scheme is a two-part scale, based on years of experience and degree held. No rationale is given for the variations in these contracts.

Some of the structures devised under collective bargaining have allowed participation in the decision-making process for academic librarians, but a similar number have perpetuated the faculty senate or committees, based on curricular units which have sometimes excluded librarians.

In summary, examination of virtually all the collective-bargaining contracts of four-year institutions has shown that although librarians have been treated equitably in a number of areas, in areas of most significance—salary, reappointment, tenure, and promotions—librarians generally have not achieved parity. While there are some indications of salary improvements for librarians, particularly in the large state systems, these improvements are usually tied to a twelve-month year rather than an academic year. Reappointment, tenure, and promotion are based on faculty standards in most instances, although peer evaluation remains central in terms of recommendations for promotion.

SUMMARY AND CONCLUSIONS

This discussion has focused on four areas. The first is enabling legislation. Academic librarians must be aware of federal and state collective-bargaining statutes. They must know how the bargaining unit is determined, who is included, and what definitions are applicable. If they are included in the bargaining unit, they must achieve high visibility, must secure key positions, must maintain informal alliances with faculty and other professionals in the unit, and must demand that the bargaining agent be sensitive to their needs.

The second area is the attitude of the collective-bargaining agent. Academic librarians must recognize that the bargaining agents on the campuses of higher-education institutions all profess to support librarians and the concept of faculty status for librarians. However, all are extremely opportunistic and political, and tend to back those groups they think will support them most effectively. Librarians must demand that these organizations and their representatives be responsive to the needs of academic librarians, through deeds as well as words.

The third area is the characteristics of higher-education institutions and faculty status. Although faculty status has been approved by most academic librarians and librarians have generally been included in the bargaining units with faculty, the narrowness with which the traditional faculty views collegiality has limited the degree to which faculty status or parity with faculty has been achieved. Collective bargaining, in and of itself, has not brought about either. Academic librarians also must recognize that higher-education institutions have characteristics that may foster or hinder collective bargaining.

The fourth area is the treatment of academic librarians in the bargaining agreement. Although academic librarians have been treated equitably in a number of respects, reappointment, tenure, and promotion seem to be the processes in which they have not achieved parity. Faculty standards are used in almost all instances.

It is hoped that the issues identified in this discussion will provide helpful insights and will enable academic librarians to assess more readily their own circumstances with regard to collective bargaining.

Conference Summary

Kenneth P. Mortimer

In this summary I shall attempt to focus some of the issues that have been discussed. In some cases I hope to add clarity; in others I must frankly admit that I cannot help you.

The first point I want to address is that a rather comprehensive set of orientation materials was prepared for this conference [see Appendix I]. In these materials are a lot of answers to common questions that have been posed. For example, there is an excellent piece on what is actually in a contract. If you read that, you will get a good idea of the scope of items that have appeared in collective-bargaining agreements.

During this conference there was some concern about what collective bargaining is and what it is not, and the discussion tended to concentrate on the *process* of negotiating an agreement, a legally binding contract. I, too, have found it useful to consider collective bargaining as a process, consisting of several stages.

The first, of course, is the unit determination stage. In that stage the first person who gets to the labor relations board or files a petition or asks an administration for recognition has the responsibility to define what his group thinks is an appropriate unit. Then anybody else can argue with that. But the impetus for defining a unit lies with the original petitioner.

There are a number of ways the unit determination process can then proceed. The administration and the petitioner can get together and agree that, indeed, they have an appropriate definition of a unit and should move ahead, subject to any dissent from that decision, or they can promptly refer it to a labor relations board to litigate their differences. That unit determination decision-making process is an extremely important one to understand.

You should also understand that there are at least four basic issues or categories of issues in the unit process. The process must determine which employees are to be in a bargaining unit. The unit is defined in the glossary [see Appendix I]. It is *not* the union. A bargaining unit is that group of people who are eligible to vote in the election and who will be covered by any subsequent contract.

The first issue is which employees should be in the unit. Do non-teaching professionals share a community of interest with faculty? What about part-timers? What about librarians? These are basic questions that must be decided.

The second issue is who is management. Remember that there are three categories of managers. The first consists of those who have assumed the title—and the president is never going to be a member of a faculty bargaining unit. Even if he only makes recommendations to the governing board, his mere title precludes his being in the faculty unit. There are also other titles, like vice president and dean, which normally exempt individuals merely because they hold those titles. No board is going to examine what they do.

There are questions, of course, about titles such as department chairman and assistant dean. While some people are excluded from a unit merely because of a title, others may be out because they perform supervisory functions. The common criterion is that their recommendations are effective, which is very nebulous terminology. One may also be exempted by being designated a confidential employee.

The question of who is management, then, or who is excluded from the unit, is an important one.

The third unit determination issue is geography. In a multicampus unit, which campuses will or will not be linked in a unit? This issue has already been extensively discussed.

The fourth issue is professional schools and their place in a large university. Do the law school and medical faculty share a community of interest with the larger faculty bargaining unit, or should they be separated for their own purposes?

A fifth question in the unit determination stage is now a dead issue. Is the faculty, in consideration of its management function, properly a group that is subject to collective bargaining? A number of courts have litigated that issue, and the answer is of course they are. The faculty is not management for collective-bargaining purposes.

The first stage of the collective-bargaining process, then, is the unit determination stage. The second stage is the election. Presumably, if a unit is defined and the board determines that at least 30 percent of that unit wants an election, the board will order it. Campaign promises fly around and people call each other all kinds of names. At that point the major associations will try to differentiate among themselves.

During the panel presentation we had a rather collegial discussion, and it was very difficult to find out where each association stands. Nationally, of course, they are not in a position of issuing a lot of policy statements, except that the AAUP has a number of such statements. In a local campaign, however, each association is going to say that the others are not like us. You will get some really hot discussion.

The third stage of the process—presuming some agent wins an election—is the negotiation of a contract. Incidentally, in four-year colleges and universities about 25 to 30 percent of the elections have resulted in a "no representative" victory. That is an important statistic. In other words, the agents do not always win.

The collective-bargaining process requires that both parties negotiate in good faith. It is very difficult for me to state what good faith means, but it *does* have a meaning. The lawyers—and that is where you need your lawyers—will advise you when you are bargaining in good faith and when you are not.

The second aspect of that negotiation process is that a legally binding document is signed. There are some people who are negotiating under *meet-and-discuss* provisions that do not require signing a legally binding document. In such cases there is usually protracted discussion. Under a meet-and-discuss provision, management is not under an obligation to make an agreement. It only has to meet and discuss.

The fourth stage of the process is the administration of the agreement, which, of course, leads to a new set of demands. That is the grievance and arbitration process, or living with a contract, and what I would call the feedback cycle, which leads into a set of new demands at the next stage of the negotiation process.

A second category of summary comments that I want to make is relative to governance. We had an excellent discussion of that topic by Don Wollett.

The best source for concepts of governance is in a report in which Don Wollett participated: *Faculty Participation in Academic Governance.*[1] It is now eight years old, but it sets up a continuum of govern-

1. *Report of the AAHE-NEA Task Force on Faculty Representation and Academic Negotiations, Campus Governance Program* (Washington, D.C.: American Association for Higher Education, National Education Association, 1967).

ance relationships from administrative dominance at one end to faculty dominance at the other, with shared authority in the middle.

The report observes that there can be agreement in an institution to share authority on some issues and to separate jurisdictions on others. That is, there is a tacit recognition by both parties that faculty judgments should prevail on such issues as grading.

That understanding may extend to other areas, such as who is to get hired, who is to get promoted, and what the salaries of individual faculty members should be. There can then be an agreement to separate jurisdictions and to make either administrative or faculty judgment prevail on given issues. On other issues there can be an agreement that joint participation is to be the style of operation. In that case the administration decides, but the influence of the faculty is effective.

Collective bargaining can be part of that scheme. Collective bargaining can legally mandate a system of joint participation or a system of separate jurisdiction. It is within that tradition when it deals with governance. I see no reason why collective bargaining must be considered different from the tradition of academic governance in this respect.

For example, if you were a faculty member or librarian at the State University of New York at Buffalo, you would be confronted by a collage of mechanisms through which you could participate in governance. If you were an administrator, there would be a collage of mechanisms with which you would have to deal on a variety of issues. SUNY's Buffalo Center has a faculty senate, a professional staff senate, and a student senate. In addition it has a collective-bargaining unit for faculty and professional staff and other units for civil service and maintenance workers. For a brief period it also had a university assembly composed of a variety of constituents: students, faculty, nonteaching professionals, and staff.

Governance, then, if you were trying to trace it at the State University of New York at Buffalo, would be a very complex collage of decisions or, in some cases, influence processes affected by a number of these mechanisms. Governance is a system of interaction which involves a number of mechanisms. Collective bargaining may be only one of them on a given campus.

The third general area on which I wish to comment is one that Gwendolyn Cruzat mentioned, that is, the special nature of universities. The fundamental issue is the faculty's professional autonomy or lack thereof and the central role of the professorial staff in delivering the product of the university. As Don Wollett noted, those privileges first reside legally in the administration, to be granted or not at the administration's discretion, absent collective bargaining. They do not extend to the majority of people employed by the university. When we talk about academic governance, we are not talking about clerks or maintenance people. We are talking about a very small proportion of the total employees of the institution, and it is important to keep that in mind.

A second point that Gwendolyn Cruzat made is that most of those institutions that are organized are community colleges (60%) and former state teachers' colleges (20%). All the literature of which I am aware indicates that these institutions, as a class, are administratively dominated. They are not characterized by the shared authority systems that one would find at the University of California at Berkeley, the University of Wisconsin at Madison, and other elite institutions. The tradition of most institutions is that of administrative domination. A relatively small number of institutions practices anything like the models of shared authority described in the literature.

In fact, I think the most important thing that one can know in judging the likely impact of collective bargaining on governance or governance on collective bargaining is the governance pattern in the institution before collective bargaining. What are the historical cultural factors? If there is a highly authoritarian administration, do not expect it to go to the table and agree to share authority overnight. If there is a relatively participative governance structure before collective bargaining, bargaining is not going to affect it very much.

Another area I wish to comment on is contract provisions. The literature indicates that at least six or seven factors are important when you are trying to judge what the provisions of a collective-bargaining agreement are likely to be. One is the law, the scope of legal bargaining. The second is the philosophy of the local association. One must also look at the history and the cultural factors of the institution and what issues are *causes célèbres*. Has any faculty member been fired in the last year, and is that likely to be a big issue at the table?

Another factor is the bargaining philosophy of the administration. Also, the composition of the bargaining unit is an extremely important factor and must be analyzed. The last factor is the personalities of the bargainers. It is very important to know if they get along, if they make deals in the hall—if it is likely to be that kind of relationship. If they hate each other, that is going to be reflected in the bargaining and in what eventually turns up in the contract.

Neil Bucklew states that bargaining philosophy can be described in three different ways. First is the comprehensive or constitutional philosophy. This appears in institutions with a history of weak governance structures, in which the collective-bargaining session develops into a constitutional convention to create governance procedures which did not exist prior to the contract.

I have recently done case studies in the Massachusetts and the Pennsylvania state colleges and I can say with some authority that those institutions do not have, and never did have, a tradition of faculty involvement in their governance. Therefore, they attempted to get it, and the administration was ready to begin to grant participation rights where they did not exist previously. In fact, the board of trustees of the State College of Massachusetts took the leadership in developing a comprehensive negotiation strategy because it wanted to hold the faculty accountable for participating in governance. It wanted the traditional system, in spite of the fact that the faculty did not have any history on which to build.

This comprehensive philosophy often spells out the criteria by which decisions are to be made. Evaluation procedures turn up in a contract. A balance between publication, research, and teaching will be specified and the means for the evaluation of teaching also will be specified.

The second type of contract or bargaining philosophy is structural negotiations, in which an item might be dealt with in structural terms only, but there is no specific statement of the criteria to be used. For example, the calendar for promotions will be specified in the contract, but there will be no mention of the criteria to be used in arriving at the promotion decision. You might see workload treated in some contracts in the following manner: "Workloads shall at all times be reasonable." That statement allows a union to grieve if somebody believes that an excessive workload is assigned.

The third type of philosophy is employment negotiations, in which the scope of bargaining is quite limited. That is, terms and conditions of employment are narrowly defined. In this case a contract might be written in some detail on fringe benefits, sabbatical leaves, insurance policies, and similar kinds of terms. However, there is no mention of governance or tenure items or various other issues. A typical example is the Rutgers University agreement. It used to be true of the Central Michigan University agreement, but that has broadened a little in recent years.

Although generalizations in this business are not usually worth much, it might be said that the more simple the mission of the college, the more detailed the contract is likely to be. In single-campus community colleges there are contracts that look like faculty handbooks because there is an overwhelming pressure to codify the evaluation of teaching. The more complex the institution—and this might also be related to measures of quality in some cases—the more simple or narrow the scope of the contract will be.

Another set of issues I wish to summarize relates to the variety of motivations for collective bargaining. While they include more money, enhanced status, due process, and the like, David Feller has brought to your attention a major motivation for collective bargaining which does not receive adequate treatment in the literature and in our conferences. It is a desire for the preservation of the status quo ante. That is the major motivation, if I understood his earlier remarks, for the Berkeley Faculty Association. It is the major motivation for the University of Wisconsin–Madison faculty's attempt to get a favorable definition of the bargaining unit.

Under this plan, the University of Wisconsin–Madison faculty would be one unit. The University of Wisconsin–Madison professional staff would be another unit. The University of Wisconsin–Milwaukee faculty would be a third unit. The University of Wisconsin–Milwaukee professional staff would be a fourth unit—and everybody else goes in another unit. The rest of that system is presumably thrown into some conglomerate unit.

From my observations, this bill represents the desires of the Madison and Milwaukee faculties to retain their autonomy and to protect what they consider to be a system of effective faculty influence from the erosion that would result from the conglomeration and homogenization effects of squeezing people into more comprehrensive bargaining units.

Indeed, the motivations for faculty bargaining are quite variable. In our own studies of faculty voting behavior we surveyed the faculty at Temple University and in the Pennsylvania State Colleges immediately after the collective-bargaining elections. The state college faculties clearly were concerned about, and wanted leverage with, the state legislature and the governor. They ranked this as the major motivation for their support for collective bargaining and influence over their choice of agent. The Temple faculty, on the other hand, was very much concerned that the president of that institution had not treated them well.

I wish to conclude by trying to summarize some of the conventional wisdom about what librarians should do when they are confronted with this collage of wisdom and lack of conclusions about collective bargaining.

First, I would urge you to look into the possibilities of stimulating, on the part of the national centers that are studying collective bargaining, special interest in codifying the experience that librarians have had with collective bargaining. In 1970 Don Wollett recommended a national clearing house on collective bargaining, of which there are now two. College and research librarians should establish contact with the National Center for the Study of Collective Bargaining in Higher Education and with the Academic Collective Bargaining Information Service in order to stimulate special interest in the status of librarians and to provide information so that librarians can get answers to questions about their situation and not have to rely on what individual researchers might know. You will then have a more objective and, I hope, codified base from which to get your information.

Second, in my view it would be the height of folly for librarians to go it alone. Collective bargaining is extremely political. You have to ask yourself what your power position is. Who would care if librarians went on strike? That is the ultimate step, about which you can make your own judgments. The alliances you can make with faculty and with associations, if you're going to contemplate collective bargaining, seem to be the most productive route to explore. To be isolated from the faculty seems to me to have major implications for your entire fight for faculty status. If you are going to separate yourselves from the teaching faculty for the purposes of collective bargaining, you have, in my judgment, lost that battle.

The third thing I would urge you to do is realize that any voluntary group, such as a union, can be dominated by a well-organized, energetic minority. The tyranny of a minority can operate in voluntary groups. Union politics are controlled by dues-paying members rather than by members of the bargaining unit. It is quite common that a union has only 30 percent membership in the unit it represents. Thus a well-organized, energetic minority within that structure can have great influence on the positions taken by the association and on the positions won at the bargaining table. I urge you to consider that strategy.

Finally, look carefully at the people, the individuals, who are trying to organize you, not at the association. AAUP, AFT, and NEA can argue with each other nationally, but when you get to the local level the crucial element is the individuals and what they stand for on the local campus.

In recent case studies we found a chapter of the AFT which is clearly in league with management on the question of what belongs in a contract. Ordinarily, you would think of AFT as a militant organization, but the institution has been organized for about six years and the local conditions have built to the point where the union is now interested in stabilizing its position at that campus, because it is in power.

In short, I do not believe that national policies control local deliberations. Look carefully, then, at the people who are trying to organize you.

You have had a very high-powered conference on collective bargaining. I am sure you will get much more from this conference as you read the proceedings than from sitting here and listening to all of us talk at you.

Background Papers

Included in this Appendix are documents selected from the materials provided to conference registrants. Although the documents come from a variety of sources, they were all identified by the Academic Collective Bargaining Information Service as particularly useful introductory materials on collective bargaining.

GLOSSARY OF LABOR TERMS

The current language of labor relations in the United States reflects the later steps on a transitional stage.

Many of the words used in describing events arising from the employer-employee relationship took on their present meaning in an environment of conflict, often breaking out into a form of private warfare.

The newer words are mainly those closely associated with the language of laws and governmental agencies. They bear witness to an increasing element of governmental regulation to replace the more or less open hostility of earlier days.

The definitions which follow are intended as a guide in the understanding of talk or writing on industrial relations.

Reprinted by permission from *Primer of Labor Relations* (20th ed.; Washington, D.C.: Bureau of National Affairs, 1975), p. 123–37.

117

Many of the words have generally understood meanings outside of their usage in the labor field. In this glossary, however, only those meanings are given which are peculiar to their usage in labor relations.

Administrative law judge—Official who conducts hearings and makes recommendations to the NLRB or other government agency. (Formerly called a trial or hearing examiner.)

Affecting commerce—Test of application of the Taft-Hartley Act. If a business is such that a labor dispute would threaten interruption of or burden interstate commerce, the jurisdiction of the National Labor Relations Board comes into play.

Affirmative order—Command issued by a labor relations board requiring the persons found to have engaged in unfair labor practices to take such steps as will, so far as possible, undo the effect of such practices.

Agency shop—A contract requiring nonmembers of the contracting union to pay to the union or a designated charity a sum equal to union dues.

Agent—Person acting for an employer or a union; act of the agent implicates the principal for whom the agent acts in the matter of unfair labor practices or of conduct subject to court action whether or not specifically authorized or approved.

Agent provocateur—Person hired to provoke industrial strike for the purpose of weakening a union.

All-union shop—A term sometimes applied to arrangement more specifically described by the terms closed shop or union shop. See *Closed shop, Union shop.*

Annual improvement factor—Annual wage increase, fixed in advance as to amount, and granted on the premise that the employees are entitled to share in the long-term increase in the productivity of a company or industry.

Annual wage—Wages paid under terms that guarantee a specified minimum for the year or a minimum period of employment for the year.

Anticertification strike—Strike designed to force an employer to cease recognizing a union which has been certified as bargaining agent and to recognize the striking union instead. This is an unfair labor practice under the Taft-Hartley Act as to which a court injunction must be asked if it is believed that a complaint should be issued.

Anti-Closed-Shop Laws—See *Right to work.*

Anti-Injunction Acts—Federal and state statutes that limit the jurisdiction of courts to issue injunctions in labor disputes. See *Injunction.*

Antitrust Laws—Federal and state statutes to protect trade and commerce from unlawful restraints and monopolies. For many years, they were used to restrict union activities such as strikes, picketing, and boycotts. In recent years, however, their use in labor cases has been limited by statute and judicial interpretation.

Appropriate unit—See *Unit.*

Arbitration—Method of deciding a controversy under which parties to the controversy have agreed in advance to accept the award of a third party.

Authorization card—Statement signed by employee designating a union as authorized to act as his agent in collective bargaining.

Automation—Term used by industrial engineers to describe mechanical materials handling and the new computer technology that can automate entire factories. It sometimes is used loosely to describe any technological improvement.

Back pay—Wages required to be paid to employees who have been discharged in violation of a legal right, either one based on a law or acquired by contract.

Back-to-work movement—Organized effort to reopen a struck plant, participated in by employees opposed to the strike and by the business community, sometimes with police aid.

Bargaining unit—See *Unit.*

Blacklist—List of names of persons or firms to be discriminated against, either in the matter of employment or patronage. See *Unfair list.*

Board of inquiry—Body to be appointed by President to mediate and report in national-emergency disputes under the Taft-Hartley Act.

Bona fide union—A union chosen or organized freely by employees without unlawful influence on the part of their employer.

Bureau of Labor Statistics—Bureau in the Labor Department that issues statistics affecting labor relations, including the Consumer Price Index to which some wage adjustments are tied.

Bootleg contract—A collective bargaining agreement which is contrary to the policy of the Taft-Hartley Act, such as a closed shop. Enforcement of such contracts may eventually entail back-pay awards, but this risk is sometimes considered, outweighed by the advantages of avoiding a strike.

Boycott—Refusal to deal with or buy the products of a business as a means of exerting pressure in a labor dispute.

Business agent—Paid representative of a local union who handles its grievance actions and negotiates with employers, enrolling of new members, and other membership and general business affairs. Sometimes called a walking delegate.

Captive audience—Employees required to attend a meeting in which an employer makes an anti-union speech shortly before an election. Now an employer need give the union an opportunity to answer such a speech under similar conditions only if he enforces a broad no-solicitation rule.

Card check—Checking union authorization cards signed by employees against employer's payroll to determine whether union represents a majority of the employer's employees.

Casual workers—Persons irregularly employed.

Cease-and-desist order—Command issued by a labor relations board requiring employer or union to abstain from unfair labor practice.

Central labor union—Federation of union locals in one city or county having affiliations with different national unions but same parent body.

Certification—Official designation by a labor board of a labor organization entitled to bargain as exclusive representative of employees in a certain unit. See *Unit.*

Charge—Formal allegations against employer or union under labor relations acts on the basis of which, if substantiated, a complaint may be issued by the board or commission.

Checkoff—Arrangement under which an employer deducts from pay of employees the amount of union dues and turns over the proceeds to the treasurer of the union.

Closed shop—Arrangement between an employer and a union under which only members of the union may be hired. See *Union shop.*

Coalition (Coordinated) bargaining—Joint or cooperative efforts by a group of unions in negotiating contracts with an employer who deals with a number of unions.

Coercion—Economic or other pressure exerted by an employer to prevent the free exercise by employees of their right to self-organization and collective bargaining; intimidation by union or fellow employees to compel affiliation with union.

Collective bargaining—Negotiations looking toward a labor contract between an organization of employees and their employer or employers.

Collective bargaining contract—Formal agreement over wages, hours, and conditions of employment entered into between an employer or group of employers and one or more unions representing employees of the employers.

Company police—Deputized police officers paid by an employer to protect his premises but used also at times to combat strikers or pickets.

Company town—Towns in which the land and houses are owned by a company which is the sole or chief employer in the town.

Company union—Organizations of employees of a single employer usually with implication of employer domination.

Concerted activities—Activities undertaken jointly by employees for the purpose of union organization, collective bargaining, or other mutual aid or protection. Such activities are "protected" under the Taft-Hartley Act.

Conciliation—Efforts by third party toward the accommodation of opposing viewpoints in a labor dispute so as to effect a voluntary settlement.

Consent decree—Court order entered with the consent of the parties.

Consent election—Election held by a labor board after informal hearing in which various parties agree on terms under which the election is to be held.

Constructive discharge—Unfavorable treatment of employee marked for discharge so that employee will "voluntarily" resign.

Consumer picketing—Picketing of a retail store in which the pickets urge customers not to patronize the store or to buy a particular product. If the picketing is in support of a strike against a producer or supplier, the picketing is legal if it is aimed merely at getting customers not to buy products of the struck employer. It is unlawful if it is aimed at getting the customers to stop patronizing the store entirely.

Consumer Price Index—An index prepared monthly by the Labor Department's Bureau of Labor Statistics measuring changes in prices of a specific "market basket" of commodities and services. It is significant in labor relations because wage escalation under some collective bargaining contracts is tied to the index.

Contract-bar rules—Rules applied by the NLRB in determining when an existing contract between an employer and a union will bar a representation election sought by a rival union.

Contracting out—See *Subcontracting*.

Cooling-off period—Period during which employees are forbidden to strike under laws which require a definite period of notice before a walkout.

Craft union—Labor organization admitting to membership persons engaged in a specified type of work, usually involving a special skill.

Craft unit—Bargaining unit consisting of workers following a particular craft or using a particular type of skill, such as molders, carpenters, etc.

Damage suits—Suits which may be brought in federal courts, without the usual limitations, to recover damages for breach of collective bargaining contracts and for violation of prohibitions against secondary boycotts and other unlawful strike action under the Taft-Hartley Act.

Deauthorization election—Election held by the NLRB under the Taft-Hartley Act to determine whether employees wish to deprive their union bargaining agent of authority to bind them under a union-shop contract.

Decertification—Withdrawal of bargaining agency from union upon vote by employees in unit that they no longer wish to be represented by union.

Discharge—Permanent separation of employee from payroll by employer.

Discrimination—Short form for "discrimination in regard to hire or tenure of employment as a means of encouraging or discouraging membership in a labor organization"; also refusal to hire, promote, or admit to union membership because of race, creed, color, sex, or national origin.

Discriminatory discharge—Discharge for union activity, or because of race, color, religion, sex, or national origin.

Domination—Control exercised by an employer over a union of his employees.

Dual union—Labor organization formed to enlist members among workers already claimed by another union.

Economic strike—Strike not caused by unfair labor practice of an employer.

Election—See *Employee election*.

Emergency board—Body appointed under Railway Labor Act by President of the United States when a strike or lockout is imminent on interstate railroads. See *Board of inquiry*.

Emergency dispute—A labor dispute in which a strike would imperil the national health and safety. Special procedures are provided under the Taft-Hartley Act for dealing with such disputes.

Employee association—Term sometimes used for plant union.

Employee election—Balloting by employees for the purpose of choosing a bargaining agent or unseating one previously recognized. See *Referendum*.

Employee representation plan—System under which employees select representatives to a joint body on which the management is also represented, the purpose of the body being to discuss grievances or company policy.

Employer association—Organization of employers in related enterprises, usually acting together in labor policy or bargaining as a unit with one or more unions.

Employer unit—Bargaining unit consisting of all production and maintenance employees working for one employer.

Employment contract—Agreement entered into between an employer and one or more employees. See *Collective bargaining contract, Individual contract*.

Equal Employment Opportunity Act of 1972—Act giving Equal Employment Opportunity Commission authority to sue in federal courts where it finds reasonable cause to believe that there has been employment discrimination based on race, color, religion, sex, or national origin.

Escalator clause—Clause in collective bargaining contract requiring wage or salary adjustments at stated intervals in a ratio to changes in the Consumer Price Index.

Escape period—A period, normally 15 days, during which employees may resign from a union so as not to be bound to continue membership under membership-maintenance agreements.

Espionage—Practice of spying on employees with a view to discovering membership in, or activity for, labor organizations.

Exactions—Payment under more or less direct duress for work not done and not intended to be done. Under the Taft-Hartley Act, seeking exactions is an unfair labor practice and making or receiving such payments is a crime for employers and unions or individuals.

Extortionate picketing—Picketing for the personal profit or enrichment of an individual, except through a bona fide increase in wages or other employee benefits, by taking or obtaining any money or other thing of value from the employer against his will or with his consent. Such picketing was made a federal crime by the Labor-Management Reporting and Disclosure Act.

Fact-finding boards—Agencies appointed, usually by a government official, to determine facts and make recommendations in major disputes. See *Board of inquiry.*

Fair employment practice—Term applied in some statutes to conduct which does not contravene prohibitions against discrimination in employment because of race, color, religion, sex, or national origin.

Featherbedding—Contractual requirements that employees be hired in jobs for which their services are not needed. See *Exactions.*

Fink—One who makes a career of taking employment in struck plants or of acting as a strike breaker, strike guard, or slugger.

Free riders—A term sometimes applied by unions to nonmembers within the unit represented by the union, the implication being that they obtain without cost the benefits of a contract obtained through the efforts of the dues-paying members.

Free speech—The right of employers to express views hostile to unionization, provided no threat of coercion or promise of benefit is contained therein. If the expression of views is coercive, it becomes unlawful interference with employees' rights.

Freeze Order—Government order freezing wages, salaries, prices, and rents as of a particular date, such as issued during the Korean War and in August 1971.

Fringe benefits—Term used to encompass items such as vacations, holidays, insurance, medical benefits, pensions, and other similar benefits that are given to an employee under his employment or union contract in addition to direct wages.

Furlough—Period of layoff.

General Counsel—Officer of the National Labor Relations Board whose chief duty is to issue and prosecute complaints in unfair labor practice cases presented to the Board for decision.

Good-faith bargaining—The type of bargaining an employer and a majority union must engage in to meet their bargaining obligation under the Taft-Hartley Act. The parties are required to meet at reasonable times and to confer in good faith with respect to wages, hours, and other terms and conditions of employment. But neither party is required to agree to a proposal or to make a concession.

Goon—Plugugly employed in labor dispute for the purpose of using or resisting violence.

Gorilla—Physically powerful person employed in labor disputes where violence is intended or expected.

Grievance—An employee complaint; an allegation by an employee, union, or employer that a collective bargaining contract has been violated.

Grievance committee—Committee designated by a union to meet periodically with the management to discuss grievances that have accumulated.

Guard—Plant protection employee. May not be represented by union affiliated with union of production employees under Taft-Hartley Act.

Hiring Hall—Place where workers are recruited for ships or waterfront activities or for work on construction projects.

Homework—Piecework performed by workers in their own homes.

Hooking—Entrapping an employee into spying on fellow employees. Usually accomplished by approaching the prospective hooked man under a pretext and engaging him to write reports.

Hot goods—Term applied by union members to products of plants employing strikebreakers, nonunion workers, or other workers regarded as hostile by union. Hot-goods or hot-cargo clauses under which a union gets an employer to agree not to require his employees to handle or work on hot goods or cargo were outlawed by one of the 1959 amendments to the Taft-Hartley Act.

Immunity clause—Clause in a contract designed to protect a union from suits for contract violation growing out of unauthorized strikes. A typical clause would limit recourse of the parties to the grievance procedure of the contract.

Impartial umpire—Person designated by agreement between a union and an employer or association of employers whose duty it is to arbitrate grievances or controversies arising under a contract.

Independent union—Local labor organization not affiliated with a national organized union; union not affiliated with a national federation of unions.

Individual contract—Agreement of employer with individual employee covering conditions of work.

Industrial union—Labor organization admitting to membership all persons employed in a plant or industry, regardless of kind of work performed.

Industrial union council—Term used by CIO as equivalent to AFL term central labor union. See *Central labor union.*

Industrial unit—Bargaining unit composed of all production and maintenance workers in one or more plants, irrespective of the type of work done.

Informational picketing—Picketing for the purpose of advising the public, including other union members, that the picketed employer does not have a union contract or is selling goods produced by a struck or nonunion employer. The 1959 amendments to the Taft-Hartley Act placed restrictions on such picketing.

Initiation fees—Fees required by unions as a condition to the privilege of becoming members. If such fees are excessive or discriminatory, an employer may not be held to the obligation under a union shop of discharging employees who do not join the union.

Injunction—Mandatory order by a court to perform or cease a specified activity usually on the ground that otherwise the complaining party will suffer irreparable injury from unlawful actions of the other party.

Inside man—Spy placed in a plant as an employee.

Inside union—Plant union without outside affiliation.

Inspector—Euphemism used to refer to spies in accounts, correspondence, etc.

Interference—Short-cut expression for "interference with the right of employees to self-organization and to bargain collectively."

International union—Nationally organized union having locals in another country, usually Canada.

Intimidation—Actual or implied threats to induce employees to refrain from joining or to join in labor organization; threats used in other aspects of labor controversies, such as picketing.

Joint council—Body established in some industries consisting of representatives of union and of employer association, its purposes being the settlement of disputes arising under a contract; body representing several craft unions in a plant or plants acting as a unit in collective bargaining.

Judicial review—Proceedings before courts for enforcement or setting aside of orders of labor relations boards. Review is limited to conclusions of law, excluding findings or fact unless these are unsupported by evidence.

Jurisdiction—Right claimed by union to organize class of employees without competition from any other union; province within which any agency or court is authorized to act. See *Work jurisdiction*.

Jurisdictional dispute—Controversy between two unions over the right to organize a given class or group of employees or to have members employed on a specific type of work.

Jurisdictional strike—A strike called to compel an employer to assign work to one class or craft of employees rather than to another. This is an unfair labor practice under the Taft-Hartley Act and may bring the question as to proper work assignment to the Labor Board for final decision.

Kickback—Return of a portion of wages paid, usually in pursuance of an undisclosed agreement with the person who hires the employee.

Labor contract—Agreement entered into between an employer and an organization of his employees covering wages, hours, and conditions of labor.

Labor dispute—As used in Norris-LaGuardia Act, a controversy involving persons in the same occupations or having interest therein or who work for the same employer or employers or who are members of the same or an affiliated union.

Labor Management Relations Act, 1947—Basic law regulating labor relations of firms whose business affects interstate commerce. It became law over the President's veto on June 23, 1947.

Labor-Management Reporting and Disclosure Act—Statute adopted in 1959 that established code of conduct for unions, union officers, employers, and labor relations consultants. It also made some significant amendments to the Taft-Hartley Act. Also popularly known as Landrum-Griffin Act.

Labor relations board—Quasi-judicial agency set up under National or State Labor Relations Acts whose duty it is to issue and adjudicate complaints alleging unfair labor practices; to require such practices to be stopped; and to certify bargaining agents for employees.

Layoff—Dropping a worker temporarily from the pay roll, usually during a period of slack work, the intention being to rehire him when he is needed.

Local—Group of organized employees holding a charter from a national or international labor organization. A local is usually confined to union members in one plant or one small locality.

Lockout—Closing down of a business as a form of economic pressure upon employees to enforce acceptance of employer's terms, or to prevent whipsawing where union bargains with an association of employers.

Lodge—Term used in some labor organizations as the equivalent of Local. See *Local.*

Loyal worker—Employee who refuses to join outside labor organization or to participate in strike. Term used by employer.

Maintenance of membership—Union-security agreement under which employees who are members of a union on specified date, or thereafter become members, are required to remain members during the term of the contract as a condition of employment.

Majority rule—Rule that the representative chosen by the majority of employees in an appropriate unit shall be the exclusive bargaining agent for all the employees.

Make-whole order—Order issued by the NLRB requiring an employer who has refused to bargain in good faith under the Taft-Hartley Act to reimburse the employees for increased wages and other benefits they would have obtained had the employer bargained in good faith. The legality of such an order is in dispute.

Management-rights clause—Collective bargaining contract clause that expressly reserves to management certain rights and specifies that the exercise of those rights shall not be subject to the grievance procedure or arbitration.

Mandatory injunction—Term applied to injunctions that the NLRB General Counsel is required to seek in the case of alleged unfair practices involving secondary boycotts, secondary-recognition strikes, recognition or organizational picketing, or strikes to force an employer to ignore an NLRB certification. Injunction remains in effect pending decision by the NLRB on the merits of the case.

Mediation—Offer of good offices to parties to a dispute as an equal friend of each; differs from conciliation in that mediator makes proposals for settlement of the dispute that have not been made by either party.

Mediation Service—Short form for Federal Mediation and Conciliation Service, which has a functional part in settlement of disputes under the Taft-Hartley Act.

Membership maintenance—Requirement under which employees who are members of the contracting union or who become so must remain members during the life of the contract as a condition of employment.

Militarized guard—Plant guard under authority of armed services in factories where work is being done under contract with armed services. Militarized guards are on payroll of factory.

Missionary—Spy whose chief work is to spread antiunion or antistrike propaganda in the general neighborhood of a plant and particularly among the wives of workers. Usually not employed in the plant.

Mohawk Valley Formula—Strategy of strike-breaking involving a combination of direct methods with organizing of antiunion sentiment and devices for undermining the morale of strikers.

Moonlighting—Practice of holding down two or more jobs at once, the second one usually being on a night shift. The Bureau of Labor Statistics estimates that 10 percent of the work force engages in this practice.

Multiple employer unit—Bargaining unit consisting of all production and maintenance workers employed by more than one employer.

Multiple plant unit—Bargaining unit consisting of all production and maintenance workers in two or more plants among a larger number owned by one employer.

National Labor Relations Act—Act passed July 5, 1935, known popularly as Wagner Act; amended form of the same incorporated as Title I of the Labor Management Relations Act, 1947, which became law June 23, 1947; also amended by Title VII of the Landrum-Griffin Act in 1959.

National Mediation Board—Agency set up under the Railway Labor Act to mediate in case of labor disputes in railroad and air transport industry and to conduct elections for choice of bargaining agents.

National Railroad Adjustment Board—Agency set up under the Railway Labor Act to settle disputes in railroad industry arising out of grievances or application of contracts.

Negotiating committee—Committee of a union or an employer selected to negotiate a collective bargaining contract.

Norris-LaGuardia Act—Popular name for Federal Anti-Injunction Act, approved Mar. 23, 1932.

Occupational Safety and Health Act—Law adopted in 1970 giving the Federal Government authority to prescribe and enforce safety and health standards in most industries.

Open Shop—Plant where employees are declared by the employer to be free to join or not join any union; the opposite number of union or closed shop.

Operative—A spy employed by an agency, usually having a secret designation.

Organizational picketing—Picketing of an employer in an attempt to induce the employees to join the union.

Outlawed strike—Strike forbidden by law. See *Unauthorized strike*.

Outside man—Spy under a cover but not masquerading as an employee in a plant. See *Missionary*.

Outside union—Nationally organized union seeking to organize workers in a plant previously unorganized or organized in a plant union.

Overtime—Period worked in excess of a standard workday or workweek, for which time a wage rate above the standard is usually paid; money received for overtime work.

Paper jurisdiction—Claim of a union to organizational rights over a certain class of employees when actually no attempt has been made to organize them.

Paper local—A local union issued a charter by the parent organization before any members have been enrolled in the local. Paper locals figured in a joint board election investigated by the McClellan Committee, the votes of the paper locals having been used to swing the election.

Picketing—Advertising, usually by members of a union carrying signs, the existence of a labor dispute and the union's version of its merits.

Piecework—Work done for wages based on output rather than on time spent.

Plant union—Organization of employees confined to one plant or factory.

Plant unit—Bargaining unit consisting of all production and maintenance workers in a plant regardless of type of work performed.

Political expenditures—Money spent by unions or corporations in connection with the nomination or election of federal officials. Such expenditures are forbidden by the Federal Corrupt Practices Act unless, in the case of unions, they are made from "voluntary" contributions of union members.

Preferential shop—Arrangement with a union under which employer agrees to give certain preferences to union members in the matter of hiring or to require that a certain proportion of employees be members of the union.

Professional employee—Employees qualifying as "professional" under Sec. 2(12) of the Taft-Hartley Act. They may not be included in a unit containing nonprofessional employees unless they so elect.

Publicity picketing—Another term for picketing aimed at publicizing a labor dispute. See *Informational picketing*.

Racketeer—Union official who uses his position to extort money from employers, usually by threatening to cause a strike.

Railway Labor Act—A federal law establishing administrative bodies and procedures for the prompt and orderly settlement of labor disputes between interstate carriers by rail and air and their employees and guaranteeing self-organization and collective bargaining rights to such carriers and employees.

Rank and File—Members of a union other than the officers.

Rat—Slightly stronger form of "scab." See *Scab*.

Recognition—Treating with a union as bargaining agent for employees, either for all or for those only who are members of the union.

Recognition picketing—Picketing for the object of inducing or compelling the employer to recognize the union as bargaining agent for the employer's employees. Recognition picketing conducted under certain circumstances was made an unfair labor practice by the 1959 amendments to the Taft-Hartley Act.

Referendum—Special election under some state laws in which employees are polled on question whether they wish to authorize their bargaining agent to sign a union-security contract or to rescind such authority previously granted.

Regional Director—Official of the National Labor Relations Board who acts for the Board in a specified region.

Reinstatement—Return to employment of persons unlawfully discharged.

Remedial order—See *Affirmative order*.

Representation election—See *Employee election*.

Restraint and coercion—Term used in Section 8(b) (1) of Taft-Hartley Act making it an unfair labor practice for a union to restrain or coerce employees in the exercise of their rights to join unions or to engage in union activities or in the exercise of their rights to refrain from joining unions or engaging in such activities.

Right to work—A term used to describe laws which ban union-security agreements by forbidding contracts making employment conditional on membership or nonmembership in labor organizations.

Roping—Securing information by striking up acquaintance or friendship with union men.

Run-away shop—Plant moved by employer to avoid bargaining with a union representing his employees.

Run-off election—Second employee election directed by a labor board when the first fails to show more than half the votes recorded for any one choice presented.

Sabotage—Malicious damage done by employee to employer's equipment or other property.

Scab—Epithet applied to nonstriking employee by fellow employees on strike, carrying significance of "traitor."

Secondary boycott—Refusal to deal with or buy goods from a concern which is the customer or supplier of an employer with whom the boycotters have a dispute. An indirect pressure is thus brought upon the primary object of the boycott.

Secondary strike—A strike against an employer to force him to use pressure upon another employer, usually a supplier or customer, to induce the other employer to accede to demands of the union upon him.

Self-organization—Self-determined activity by employees in the formation of labor unions.

Seniority—Length of service with an employer or in one branch of a business; preference accorded employees on the basis of length of service.

Settlement agreement—Terms agreed upon in the settlement of charges before the NLRB without a full-dress hearing, decision, and order. To be binding, such agreements must have the consent of the NLRB.

Shadowing—Operation of keeping a person under secret surveillance.

Share-the-work plan—Arrangement under which, in lieu of cutting payroll when the work falls off, the hours worked by each employee are shortened.

Shop steward—Person designated by a union to take up with the foreman or supervisor the grievances of fellow employees as they arise.

Shop unit—Subdivision of a union consisting of members employed in a single shop. Its affairs are ordinarily subject to decisions by a local. See *Local*.

Showing of interest—Support union must show among employees in bargaining unit before NLRB will process union's election petition. The Board requires a union that is seeking a representation election to make a showing of interest among 30 percent of the employees in the bargaining unit.

Shutdown—Temporary closing of plant, usually because of slack work or for changing plant equipment.

Sit-down strike—Stoppage of work where the strikers remain in occupancy of the employer's premises.

Slowdown—Concerted slackening of pace in working as a means of enforcing demands made by employees.

Slugger—Specialized type of fink used to attack, assault, and beat up strikers and union leaders. Generally armed. See *Fink*.

Soldiering—Deliberate slackening of pace in work, usually as a protest against uncorrected grievances.

Speed-up—Quickening the pace of operations performed by employees, usually through stepping up the speed of machines which they attend.

Statute of limitations—As applied to unfair labor practices, a provision of the Taft-Hartley Act under which charges are outlawed if based on events more than six months old.

Stool pigeon—Person acting as industrial spy and agent provocateur.

Stranger picketing—Picketing conducted by persons who are not employees of the picketed employer. It has been held unlawful under the laws of some states.

Stretch-out—Increasing work quota of employees, usually by increasing number of operations to be performed or of machines to be watched.

Strike—Concerted cessation of work as a form of economic pressure by employees, usually organized, to enforce acceptance of their terms.

Strikebreaker—One whose trade it is to take employment in struck plants. Distinguishable from "scab," who is a workman. May pretend to work in the plant or act as a guard.

Strike vote—Balloting or canvass on question of calling a strike.

Struck work—Work performed by employees of one employer that would have been performed by employees of another employer had they not been on strike.

Subcontracting—Farming out of part of a plant's work to another company. Such diversion of work for the purpose of avoiding or evading the duty to bargain with a union is an unfair labor practice under the Taft-Hartley Act.

Superseniority—Seniority granted by contract to certain classes of employees in excess of that which length of service would justify and which is protected against reduction by events which would have the effect of reducing seniority of other employees. Union stewards and veterans are sometimes accorded superseniority. The granting of superseniority to strikers' replacements has been held to be an unfair labor practice.

Supervisor—An employee with authority to hire and fire or make effective recommendations to this effect. Supervisors enjoy no protection of bargaining rights under the Taft-Hartley Act.

Supplemental unemployment benefits—Employer-financed payments to laid-off employees to supplement the state unemployment benefits they receive.

Surveillance—Keeping watch on employees to detect evidence of union activity.

Sympathetic strike—Strike called for the purpose of influencing outcome of a dispute in another enterprise or industry.

Taft-Hartley Act—Popular name of Labor Management Relations Act, 1947, which became law June 23, 1947. Title I consists of the National Labor Relations Act as amended in 1947.

Unauthorized strike—A strike by employees contrary to the advice or without the consent of their union.

Unfair employment practice—Discrimination in employment based on race, color, religion, sex, or national origin. Forbidden by federal and some state laws.

Unfair labor practice—Practice forbidden by the National and several State Labor Relations Acts.

Unfair labor practice strike—Strike caused or prolonged in whole or in part by the employer's unfair labor practices. In such a strike, the employer must reinstate the strikers in their jobs, upon unconditional application, even though it is necessary to let replacements go.

Unfair list—Names of employers publicized by unions as "unfair" because of their refusal to recognize the union or because of some other dispute.

Union—Labor organization.

Union hiring—System under which new employees must be chosen from among union members, the union determining the members to be taken on.

Union insignia—Buttons or other signs worn by employees to indicate that they are union members. Prohibition against their display has been held unlawful interference with organizational rights, absent unusual circumstances.

Union label—Marks placed on goods indicating that they have been made in a shop which deals with a labor union.

Union shop—Arrangement with a union by which employer may hire any employee, union or nonunion, but the new employee must join the union within a specified time and remain a member in good standing.

Unit—Shortened form of "unit appropriate for collective bargaining." It consists of all employees entitled to select a single agent to represent them in bargaining collectively.

Wagner Act—National Labor Relations Act, approved July 5, 1935. So called from its chief sponsor, Senator Robert F. Wagner, of New York.

Walkout—Strike in which workers leave the shop or plant.

Welfare and Pension Plans Disclosure Act—Federal law enacted in 1958 and amended in 1962 establishing reporting, disclosure, and regulatory requirements for employee welfare and pension plans.

Welfare plan—Arrangements with a union under which insurance and other benefits will be paid to employees and their families. Employer contributions are forbidden except under conditions laid down in Sec. 302 of the Taft-Hartley Act.

Wildcat strike—Unauthorized strike. See *Outlawed strike.*

Work jurisdiction—Right claimed by union under its charter to have its members and no others engaged in certain work. See *Jurisdictional dispute, Jurisdictional strike.*

Work permit—Card issued by union having closed shop to show permission that holder, though not a full-fledged union member, may be employed under contract.

Yellow-dog contract—Agreement under which an employee undertakes not to join a union while working for his employer.

Zipper clause—Clause that seeks to close all employment terms for the duration of the labor contract by stating that the agreement is "complete in itself" and "sets forth all terms and conditions" of the agreement.

LEGAL PRINCIPLES OF PUBLIC SECTOR BARGAINING

Russell A. Smith

In the absence of specific legislation, the applicable law concerning rights of organization and collective bargaining is derived from three sources: the common law (as expounded in judicial decisions), municipal law (basic legislation, including home rule provisions defining the powers of local government), and constitutional law. The public sector presents a different mix of elements from that prevalent in the private sector, as we shall see. Those who deal with the public sector must have a correspondingly different expertise.

The traditional view has been that public employees have no legal right to protection against the employer's interference in attempts at unionization. A countertrend may be forming, however. A few recent court decisions (so far none by the Supreme Court of the United States) have taken the view that the First Amendment guarantees the right to form or join or belong to an organization concerned with working conditions.

Suppose, then, that a body of public employees, such as a college faculty, organizes for bargaining purposes. Unless applicable legislation specifically requires public employers to bargain collectively, these people will have no legally protected right to bargain. At best they will have a *de facto* right, where the employer agrees to bargain either voluntarily or in response to pressure tactics. The traditional view of strikes is the same. Moreover, where legislation does not specifically provide it, public employees have no legal mechanism for handling representation issues (who has the right to represent particular groups of employees), for resolving impasses, or for dealing with other kinds of disputes. In such situations, attempts to organize are hampered by the lack of legal protection.

Recent Developments

A highly significant development over the past decade has been the enactment of legislation dealing with public sector unionism. Wisconsin enacted the first comprehensive legislation in 1959. Now over thirty states have done so. Comprehensive legislation covers entire categories of public employees, sometimes all categories. As a general rule, such legislation grants and protects the right of self-organization; establishes the principle that the majority determines the representative of an "appropriate" employee group; places upon the employer the legal obligation to "bargain collectively" or to "meet and confer" with an organization

Reprinted by permission from Terrence N. Tice, ed., *Faculty Power: Collective Bargaining on Campus* (Ann Arbor, Mich.: Institute of Continuing Legal Education, 1972), p. 9–22.

having representation rights; and provides for help in resolving disputes (usually mediation plus fact-finding), but prohibits strike action. A few states even provide for compulsory arbitration in certain types of disputes, principally those involving police and firefighters.

Some important changes have also occurred at the federal level. In 1962, President Kennedy issued Executive Order 10988, applying broadly to federal employees and conferring on them limited rights of unionization and collective bargaining. President Nixon has continued the same general policy, with some modifications, in Executive Order 11491, issued in 1969 and recently amended. Another interesting development is the grant of rights of unionization to postal employees under the Postal Reorganization Act of 1970[1]—rights comparable to those operative in the private sector.

Cornell University. In 1970, departing from tradition, the National Labor Relations Board (NLRB) elected to enter the field of higher education in the private sector. In the Cornell University[2] case it decided to assert jurisdiction over the University in its relationships with nonacademic employees. The NLRB has since ruled that it will assume jurisdiction over private educational institutions which have at least a million dollars of annual revenue for operating purposes.[3]

The question of whether the NLRB would extend its jurisdiction to academic employees in private institutions was soon answered. In April, 1971, the board asserted jurisdiction over two branches of Long Island University—the C. W. Post Center and the Brooklyn Center—in a representation proceeding initiated by the United Federation of College Teachers, an affiliate of the American Federation of Teachers. In one branch there was an intervening petition by the local chapter of the American Association of University Professors (AAUP).[4] The University did not contest the assumption of NLRB jurisdiction although representation of academic employees was being sought. The issues litigated concerned the scope of the bargaining units.

Fordham University. In the Fordham University[5] case in 1971, again an AAUP chapter petitioned the NLRB for certification as the bargaining representative of the entire faculty. (This is also true in the Manhattan College case, currently pending.) Fordham University hoped to persuade the board to refuse jurisdiction over faculty, if not to obtain the exclusion of large segments of the faculty from the collective bargaining unit. The board decided to assume jurisdiction. The brief presents an interesting

1. August 12, 1970, P. L. 91–375, 84 Stat. 719.
2. 183 NLRB 41.
3. 186 NLRB 153.
4. C. W. Post Center, 189 NLRB 109.
5. 193 NLRB 23.

analysis of the structure of the academic community at Fordham. Much of it is comparable to the structure of the University of Michigan.

State Legislation. The federal government has not as yet extended NLRB jurisdiction to public employees. Thus, developments at the state level are far more important in the public sector than in the private sector. This could change. Meanwhile, the considerable development that has occurred at the state level is beneficial. The states are free to do some experimenting, a valuable approach if we are to identify our problems and find ways to meet them. Experimentation is possible where a monolithic legislative structure is not imposed, as would be true if the NLRB were to assume jurisdiction over public employees as well.

In a recent seminar at The University of Michigan Law School, Chairman Robert Helsby of the New York Public Employment Relations Board usefully characterized the states in three categories: (1) The "do nothing" states have not yet faced up to the problem and are restricted to applying the principles first mentioned—the common law, municipal law, and constitutional law. Public sector employees in these states have little or no legal protection in their efforts at organization and collective bargaining. Changes can be expected soon in some of these states, notably Illinois and Ohio. (2) The "squeaky wheel" states have crisis legislation, enacted piecemeal to meet problems with teachers, police, firefighters, or municipal employees. Comprehensive legislation is lacking. Many of these statutes, in Mr. Helsby's view, grant less than full rights and fail to deal effectively with the problems that are bound to emerge. (3) The "real confrontation" states have faced up to the problems of public sector unionism and have taken a broad view, trying to decide the proper approach as a matter of overall policy. These states have more comprehensive legislation, often drawing upon the recommendations of study commissions. At least sixteen states have enacted legislation applicable to the academic community.[6]

Informed observers generally believe that unless Congress elects to step in with superseding legislation, the trend toward enactment of state legislation will continue. The probability is that within five or six years forty or more states will have enacted legislation granting rights of self-organization and collective bargaining to some or all categories of public employees. This may stimulate an already strong trend toward unionization, as was true in the private sector following enactment of the National Labor Relations Act (NLRA) in 1935.[7]

6. Connecticut, Delaware, Hawaii, Maine, Massachusetts, Michigan, Minnesota, New Jersey, New York, Oregon, Pennsylvania, Rhode Island, South Dakota. Vermont, Washington and Wisconsin.

7. National Labor Relations Act of July 5, 1935, 29 U.S.C. Sec. 151 et seq.

Remarkably, organization among public white collar and professional groups far exceeds the organization of such groups in the private sector. Obviously something is happening which appeals more strongly to public employees than to private employees.

Two Agencies? An administrative problem arises in those states which have a little Wagner Act or a little Taft-Hartley Act covering the private sector. Should the same agency administer the legislation for both sectors? New York separates the two. Michigan entrusts administration to a single agency.

Proponents of separate agencies wish to avoid the use of too many private sector concepts in the implementation of public sector legislation. They believe that public sector legislation presents unique problems calling for the undivided attention of an agency created for its specific administration—an agency not overly attuned to or influenced by decisions already made in the private sector. Proponents of a single agency claim economy of operation and assert that problems peculiar to the public sector can be identified and adequately treated.

I see benefit in the variety of approaches, state and federal, now developing. We cannot yet say exactly what we need or what we want on the statute books. We are not ready to specify the most effective kind of administration or the general principles which should govern. This is particularly true with regard to the extension of unionism to college and university faculties. We can now examine a potpourri of state legislation and experiences under that legislation. Hopefully the experimentation will enable us to identify and learn to deal with the problems peculiar to the public sector.

The Bargaining Unit

Among the important problems to be considered in enacting and administering legislation is the determination of appropriate units for collective bargaining purposes. In this country we accept the principle of majority determination within a defined group of employees and therefore deny bargaining rights to minority groups. This concept is uniquely American. We first accepted it in 1934—in an amendment to the federal Railway Labor Act of 1926 and in the administration of the National Industrial Recovery Act. The principle was incorporated in the NLRA of 1935 and continued in the Taft-Hartley Act of 1947. All state legislation has followed the same principle.

A necessary corollary of this principle is that the boundary lines of the voting group must be determined. A ruling must specify which employees may vote to decide whether they want to be represented by a particular labor organization or by one among competing labor organizations or by none. This is a key issue and the implications are obvious. For a time, at least, the decision spells life or death to the aspirations of organizations which fail to win. Moreover, the definition of the unit substantially affects the resulting bargaining structure. For example, the bargaining units might be statewide or the units might correspond to the various operating departments or even to sections of those departments. Both the employer and the management structure for bargaining obviously will have to be responsive to these alignments.

Supervisory Employees. Another problem encountered in determining bargaining units is what to do about employees having supervisory status. The NLRA defines supervisory employees very broadly and denies them statutory protection with respect to organization and collective bargaining, with the result that they may be included in a bargaining unit only with the employer's consent.[8] In the Fordham University case the University argued, on the basis of the NLRB definition, that the entire tenured faculty, who are members of the faculty senate, should be excluded from the bargaining unit in view of the varied responsibilities of the faculty regarding curriculum, appointments, promotions, grievances, supervision of graduate students and research assistants, and the like; and in view of the faculty senate's other collective managerial responsibilities in decision-making.

The argument did not prevail. Difficult questions are involved here, nonetheless. Should the private sector concepts of "supervisor" control in the academic setting? Would the traditional collegial forms of faculty participation in academic governance have to be scrapped to permit the introduction of NLRA-type collective bargaining? Should departmental chairmen, assistant deans, and members of departmental executive committees be included with the regular faculty in an appropriate bargaining unit or, state law permitting, should they be accorded bargaining rights but in separate bargaining units?

Legislative Guidelines for Unit Determination

A survey of state statutes and the federal executive orders yields a variety of approaches to the definition of an appropriate unit. Some state legislation contains language similar to that of the NLRA, providing minimal legislative guidance and leaving the standards for determining appropriate groupings of employees to the discretion of the administering

8. NLRA Sec. 2(11), 29 U.S.C. Sec. 152(11) states: "The term 'supervisor' means any individual having authority, in the interest of the employer, to hire, transfer, suspend, lay off, recall, promote, discharge, assign, reward, or discipline other employees, or responsibly to direct them, or to adjust their grievances, or effectively to recommend such action, if in connection with the foregoing the exercise of such authority is not of a merely routine or clerical nature, but requires the use of independent judgement."

agency. Other states have tried to provide specific guidelines. The Hawaii statute,[9] effective July 1, 1970, definitively prescribes bargaining units to be used statewide:

All employees throughout the State within any of the following categories shall constitute an appropriate bargaining unit: (1) Nonsupervisory employees in blue collar positions; (2) Supervisory employees in blue collar positions; (3) Nonsupervisory employees in white collar positions; (4) Supervisory employees in white collar positions; (5) Teachers and other personnel of the department of education under the same salary schedule; (6) Educational officers and other personnel of the department of education under the same salary schedule; (7) Faculty of The University of Hawaii and the community college system; (8) Personnel of The University of Hawaii and the community college system, other than faculty; (9) Registered professional nurses; (10) Nonprofessional hospital and institutional workers; (11) Firemen; (12) Policemen; and (13) Professional and scientific employees other than registered professional nurses.

Other states have not yet set such specific guidelines for bargaining units, but have indicated some preference in terms of general principles or policies. The Pennsylvania statute[10] directs the agency to avoid an over-fragmentation of bargaining units to the extent feasible, thus recognizing a problem of serious proportions.

The Scope of Negotiations

The legally permissible and desirable scope of subject matter for collective negotiations is a critical issue. The answer, of course, depends on the applicable statute and how it is interpreted.

Some state statutes are modeled after the NLRA, stating the duty to bargain "in good faith with respect to wages, hours, and other terms and conditions of employment." The NLRB and the courts have developed a substantial body of interpretations implementing those provisions. Will the state administrative agencies and the state courts tend to apply the same kinds of principles?

Some state legislatures consider the scope of bargaining in the public sector to be such a serious problem that they have attempted to exclude some subjects from the bargaining process. The Hawaii statute has the following provisions:

Excluded from the subjects of negotiations are matters of classification and reclassification, retirement benefits and the salary ranges and the number of incremental and longevity steps now provided by law, provided that the amount of wages to be paid in each range and step and the length

9. Session Laws of Hawaii, Act 171, 1970.
10. 43 Pa. Stat. Ann. Sec. 1101.101 et seq. (Purdon 1970).

of service necessary for the incremental and longevity step shall be negotiable. The employer and the exclusive representative shall not agree to any proposal which would be inconsistent with merit principles or the principle of equal pay for equal work pursuant to [another statute] or which would interfere with the rights of a public employer to (1) direct employees; (2) determine qualification, standards for work, the nature and contents of examinations, hire, promote, transfer, assign and retain employees in positions and suspend, demote, discharge, or take over disciplinary action against employees for proper cause; (3) relieve an employee from duties because of lack of work or other legitimate reasons; (4) maintain efficiency of government operation; (5) determine methods, means, and personnel by which the employer's operations are to be conducted; and take such action as may be necessary to carry out the missions of the employer in cases of emergencies.

Other statutes use different language, either mandatory or permissive. *Management Functions.* An alternative approach is to require that certain stated functions be retained by management. Thus, federal Executive Order No. 11491 states in Section 12:

Each agreement between an agency and a labor organization is subject to the following requirements: . . . (b) management officials of the agency retain the right, in accordance with applicable laws and regulations— (1) to direct employees of the agency; (2) to hire, promote, transfer, assign, and retain employees in positions within the agency, and to suspend, demote, discharge, or take other disciplinary action against employees; (3) to relieve employees from duties because of lack of work or for other legitimate reasons; (4) to maintain the efficiency of the Government operations entrusted to them; (5) to determine the methods, means, and personnel by which such operations are to be conducted; and (6) to take whatever actions may be necessary to carry out the mission of the agency in situations of emergency; . . .

The requirements of this section shall be expressly stated in the initial or basic agreement and apply to all supplemental, implementing, subsidiary, or informal agreements between the agency and the organization.

Some state statutes include similar restrictive provisions which have the effect of circumscribing public sector negotiations far more narrowly than is true in the private sector.

Conflicting Legislation. Another tough legal problem arises in administering public sector legislation where the bargaining obligation is expressed in general NLRA-type terms. A determination must be made as to the extent the bargainers are free to negotiate to finality on matters specifically covered by preexisting legislation. A state law may provide for a state-administered pension plan, or create a state-administered system of teacher tenure, or provide specific hours of work for firemen. Municipalities operating under home rule charters adopted pursuant to state constitutional authority may establish pension plans or civil service systems or otherwise deal specifically with other terms and conditions of employment regarding some or all categories of city employees. A serious question arises in these contexts: Does the enactment of legislation which states the bargaining obligation in general terms override preexisting legislation and home rule charters which have set terms and conditions of employment? These problems have already arisen, with varying results, and will continue to plague the administering agencies, the courts, and the parties to bargaining.

Some state legislation has sought to meet this problem, but the provisions are often difficult to interpret. The New York statute, for example, includes the following provision:[11]

> Any written agreement between a public employer and an employee organization determining the terms and conditions of employment of public employees shall contain the following notice in type not smaller than the largest type used elsewhere in the agreement:
>> It is agreed by and between the parties that any provision of this agreement requiring legislative action to permit its implementation by amendment by law or by providing the additional funds therefor, shall not become effective until the appropriate legislative body has given approval.

The appropriate legislative body for statewide or state employees, I would presume, is the legislature itself. The appropriate legislative body at the school district level, at least in Michigan, would be the district school board and at the municipal level in both New York and Michigan —if Michigan had the provision—the city council or a similar legislative body.

Perhaps this kind of restriction does not pose a great problem at the municipal level, since municipal government can only become bound or provide funds by appropriate legislative action, but an important technical distinction should be noted. Provisions such as those stated in the New York statute (or like provisions in the Pennsylvania statute[12] and elsewhere) may mean that the local legislative body has two bites at the apple. In statewide bargaining relationships where the bargaining is done by a subordinate agency of the state, as it certainly must be, the provision would apparently mean that the labor relations act does not necessarily circumscribe the field of negotiations. Anything could be negotiated, including pension plans covered by a state law, but the resulting agreements would lack finality. The parties would have to take the further political step of seeking confirmation from the legislature.

11. N. Y. Civil Service Law Sec. 204-a (McKinney 1969).
12. 42 Pa. Stat. Ann. Sec. 1101.901 (Purdon 1970).

That situation presents an enormous problem not faced in the private sector.

The Bargaining Obligation

What kind of bargaining or negotiation obligation is imposed by state provisions or by President Nixon's 1969 federal Executive Order 11491? The executive order and some state legislation directs that parties "meet and confer" with respect to wages, hours, and other terms and conditions of employment. The language of the NLRA, copied in many state acts, states an obligation to "bargain collectively" with respect to wages, hours, and other terms and conditions of employment. Are these obligations identical?

Presumably the use of the "meet and confer" language represents a deliberate attempt to impose a bargaining obligation less strict than the traditional obligation to "bargain collectively in good faith." I do not purport to deal here with the full ramifications of the distinction. The basic theoretical difference is that meeting and conferring, unlike the stricter bargaining, does not mandate that negotiations be carried to an impasse. It neither requires nor permits the administering agency to pass judgment on the bargaining process as minutely as the NLRB has customarily done. The NLRB examines the negotiations, often in great detail, to determine whether bargaining positions have been taken in good faith. Such examination goes substantially beyond inquiry into whether the parties have simply met and conferred.[13]

The bargaining structure is an extremely important aspect of the total bargaining process, and structure is greatly affected by determination of the appropriate bargaining unit. As fragmentation of units increases, so does the problem of conducting collective bargaining. This problem is serious in the private sector but even more serious in the public sector. What one unit gets other units will want, and probably more—a roadblock hampering the negotiation of a complete set of agreements. Unfortunately, highly fragmented bargaining units have emerged under some state laws. Other state laws encourage the establishment of broad units, with particular sensitivity to the special problems collective bargaining

13. Under the Los Angeles City Ordinance (GERR, No. 388-F-1; Jan. 1971), it is an unfair employee relations practice for either management or the union "to refuse to meet and confer in good faith at reasonable times, places, and frequencies . . . or to refuse to consult upon request . . . on matters which are within the proper scope of representation." "Meet and confer" is defined as the obligation "to meet and confer within a reasonable period of time in order to exchange freely information, opinions, and proposals, and to endeavor to reach an agreement on matters within the scope of representation."

faces in the public sector. It is to be hoped that future legislation will follow the latter course.

The bargaining structure is in some respects a practical rather than a legal problem. In theory, most legislation is formulated to prevent one side from interfering with the internal structure adopted by the other side. However, the good faith requirement can be a basis for the claim that each side should have bargaining teams possessing genuine authority to negotiate—a matter of internal structure. The size and makeup of a bargaining unit will have considerable bearing on how such authority and structure are designed.

A faculty senate or other similar decision-making body in a college or university conceivably could become the faculty's bargaining agent. Certification of an outside agent or an AAUP chapter would raise the critical question of what should be done with an existing decision-making or consultative apparatus.

The Strike Issue

In the private sector the accepted orthodoxy is that there can be no genuine collective bargaining without the right to strike. The possibility of withholding services is supposed to be the catalyst which helps to produce agreement. The employer's ability to lock out employees theoretically plays a similar role. On the other hand, the prevailing view reflected in state statutes is that strikes by public employees are illegal.

The statutes of Hawaii and Pennsylvania do not impose an absolute prohibition on all strike action, but they do provide that strikes which critically affect the public welfare are not permitted. The same is true of the Vermont statute with respect to municipal employees. Hawaii and Pennsylvania also prohibit strikes before the statutory impasse procedures have been exhausted. Pennsylvania prohibits strikes by guards at mental hospitals or prisons, by personnel necessary to the functioning of the courts, and by police and firefighters.

The state legislatures have stated the strike prohibition in various ways and with various kinds of supporting sanctions. Michigan and some other states provide no specific sanction, but the employer may take disciplinary action or seek a court injunction. In other states specific, and in some instances severe, sanctions are indicated. The New York statute mandates that injunctive relief be sought, that strikers have probationary status for one year, and that a deduction be taken from the worker's pay of an amount equal to twice his daily rate of pay for each day of violation. Further, a union in violation of the act forfeits its right to have dues deducted for a period of time to be determined by the public employment relations board; and the union may be fined for contempt of an injunctive order in an amount fixed by the court.

Injunctive relief, where available, is not necessarily automatic. The labor organization, countering with a charge of bad faith bargaining or the like (as in Michigan under the Holland[14] decision) may defeat or delay the issuance of an injunction.

Impasse Resolution

Public sector legislation emphasizes impasse resolution procedures. The usual pattern is mediation followed by fact-finding with nonbinding recommendations. Six states[15] have provided for binding arbitration of disputes with police, firefighters, or other groups.[16] Nevada recently adopted a statute giving the governor authority to direct, before submission of a dispute to fact-finding, that the recommendations on some or all issues be final and binding. The Maine and Rhode Island statutes provide for compulsory arbitration of some, but not all, issues.

The results of strikes by public employees vary with the state of the labor market, the kinds of sanctions authorized, and whether such sanctions are imposed. However, many believe that we must concentrate not on the strike issue but on developing suitable dispute settlement mechanisms.

As compared with mediation and fact-finding, compulsory arbitration is not yet extensively used. Its use raises some interesting questions. What kinds of decision standards should be applied? How important are limitations on budget or revenue sources in determining wage issues and other money issues? In effect, does arbitration involve a dangerous reallocation of governmental responsibility and authority? Does it have an adverse effect on collective bargaining? Is it desirable in part on the ground that it may substitute rationality and equity for the relative power positions of the parties to collective bargaining?

I have tried to provide a capsulized survey of the legal structure and some of the problems underlying public sector unionism at the federal and state levels, with some comparative references to the private sector. It should be obvious, even from this limited discussion, that private sector legal and structural models have strongly influenced the nature of public sector legislation and practices. That influence may lessen with increased efforts to take into account the problems peculiar to the public sector, efforts especially needed in considering how to handle the unionization of college faculties.

14. Holland v. Holland Education Association, 380 Mich. 314, 157 N.W.2d 206 (1968).

15. Maine, Michigan, Rhode Island, South Dakota, Vermont, and Wyoming.

16. Michigan's experiment with compulsory arbitration will expire in June of 1972 unless the legislature elects to extend it.

CONTRACTS

The following is an outline of provisions that may be included in a collective-bargaining agreement.

The summary is based on the *Encyclopedia of Collective Bargaining*, Harold I. Goodwin and Edwin R. Smith, West Virginia University, 1975.

Contract Management

Statement of Intent. The areas for negotiation are set out. Enforcement of the contract is the responsibility of both parties.

Should any dispute arise over the interpretation or application of the agreement, representatives of both sides will meet and confer in good faith to resolve differences. The agreement supersedes any rules, regulations, or policies of the governing board contrary to or inconsistent with its terms.

Recognition of Agent. The union is recognized, for the duration of the contract, as the sole and exclusive representative of the bargaining unit for the purposes of collective bargaining regarding such concerns as wages, hours, and terms and conditions of employment, and in the settlement of grievances and for all lawful purposes under the laws of the state and the rules of the National Labor Relations Board. The governing board agrees not to negotiate with any faculty organization or individual within the bargaining unit other than the union (although individuals may be allowed to present grievances separately, if the adjustment is not inconsistent with the terms of the agreement).

Bargaining-Unit Composition. The group which the union represents is defined. This may, for example, include only full-time faculty members of a particular professional school. It may embrace all full-time and probationary faculty above and including the rank of instructor. Or it may extend from full-time professors to assistant librarians, bookstore managers, etc. State and N.L.R.B. definitions of "administrator" are taken into consideration.

Terms and Definitions. Among the most frequently defined terms are: academic (caucus, employee, matters, position, rank, responsibilities, year, etc.); administrative (appointment, representative, unit) and administrator; bargaining unit; faculty and faculty association; full-time (faculty, non-teaching faculty, employment, etc.); grievance; probationary (faculty and faculty appointment); senior faculty and seniority; temporary (appointment, employee, faculty, etc.); tenure; termination; and working day.

Reprinted by permission from *A Chronicle of Higher Education Handbook: Faculty Collective Bargaining* (Washington, D.C.: Editorial Projects for Education, 1975), p. 8–16.

Procedures. The contract must be ratified by both the governing board and the membership of the bargaining unit.

Neither party may control or influence the selection of the other's bargaining representatives. Only the chief negotiators for each side shall request meetings, arrange the bargaining agenda, set the time and place for meetings, and serve as spokespersons in and out of the bargaining sessions.

Either chief negotiator may call a caucus at any time during a session, requiring bargaining to stop.

If agreement cannot be reached or one party refuses to negotiate on any item, either party may declare an impasse and request mediation, fact-finding, or arbitration. No details of the negotiations shall be released for publication until the agreement has been ratified.

The agreement is subject to the appropriation of necessary funds. Both parties will support any legislation required to carry out the terms of the agreement. The agreement incorporates the entire understanding between the parties on all matters that were or could have been the subject of negotiations.

Duration of Contract. Most contracts are for one year, although some are for two or three years.

Reopening Negotiations. Bargaining can be reopened during the life of the contract at the request of one party and with the consent of the other. Some contracts prohibit any reopening, except for salary schedules in multiple-year contracts.

Consultation and Communication. Periodic meetings are scheduled between management and representatives of the bargaining unit to resolve issues of concern to both parties. Such issues might include personnel management, working conditions, budget, university organization, and changes in the mission of the institution.

Distribution of Agreement. The cost of printing and distributing the agreement is almost always the governing board's obligation, but on occasion the faculty bargaining unit shares the cost.

Conformity to Law. If any provision of the contract is found by the courts to be contrary to law, it is invalid, but the rest of the contract remains in force.

General Provisions

Dues Check-Off. Procedures are established under which union dues may be deducted from a faculty member's paycheck by the institution. Often, provisions are included which allow a member of the bargaining unit to cancel the automatic check-off. Transfer of funds from the institution to the union is also provided for.

No Strike, No Lock-out. The faculty agrees not to strike, and the governing board agrees not to lock out any employees for the duration of the contract. Members of the bargaining unit who do participate in strikes are excluded from the grievance procedures of the contract.

Bargaining-Agent Rights. Provisions are made for a representative of the union to attend meetings of the governing board, or to speak to the board, or to appear on the board's agenda. Provisions may also be made for the union to receive agenda of upcoming board meetings and minutes of past meetings. Information to be furnished to the union by the board might also be specified.

Procedures allowing union representatives to meet on a regular basis with the president, deans, or other representatives of management are determined.

Regular times—often one hour each month—are set aside for union meetings. Only under extraordinary circumstances may the institution schedule conflicting meetings during this time. Office space—and often specified office equipment—are provided the union, and the use of bulletin boards and institutional mailing service is determined.

Schedule reductions for union officers are agreed upon as is union representation on standing committees.

Governance

Faculty Governance. The presently constituted governing organizations of the institution, such as faculty senates or councils, shall continue to operate, provided that no action they take can rescind or modify any provisions of the contract.

Often a general statement recognizing the value of faculty participation in institutional governance appears in the contract. Many contracts also include the entire governing organization of the college.

Committees. The types, duties, membership, and selection of committees are established. Such provisions are often quite detailed.

Management Rights. The governing board retains all rights, powers, duties, and responsibilities conferred upon it by state or federal law, or by the institution's charter.

Emergency conditions under which management may rescind or place in abeyance part or all of the terms of the agreement might be specified. Such conditions might include countermanding directives from a state board of education, retrenchment, acts of God, etc.

Selection of Administrators. Procedures for choosing administrators such as deans and department chairmen are often outlined, with special emphasis on the faculty role. Often—and particularly with regard to department chairman—management is required to produce a written explanation should it reject the nomination of a faculty committee.

Duties of Department Chairmen. The duties are outlined. Often such specifications include a reduced teaching load and may provide for an additional stipend.

Maintenance of Benefits and Rights. All well-established, generally applicable practices which benefit members of the bargaining unit in a significant manner are maintained, unless modified by the collective-bargaining agreement or by mutual consent of management and union.

Personnel Policies

General. Each faculty member is entitled to due process. Policies shall be applied without discrimination. The faculty handbook shall be amended to conform to the contract. Legal responsibility for implementation might be assigned to the governing board.

Personnel Files. Conditions are provided under which a faculty member may see his or her personnel file, although some material, such as references from sources outside the college, may be excluded. The type of material that may be included in a personnel file is enumerated, often with the provision that the faculty member may add material to his or her own file. Occasionally, employers are forbidden to include records of grievance procedures in the official files. Procedures are provided for removing material from the file.

Specification of who has access to an employee's file—and under what conditions—is made. Often included is further specification of what materials from the official file may be used against the employee.

Grievance Procedures. Grievances are defined and procedures set out for appealing them, often involving multiple steps—informal and formal. Final appeal may be to the board or to an outside arbitrator, whose powers and authority are defined. Guarantees of no reprisal and right to counsel or other representation are given by management.

Anti-Discrimination. The bargaining agent agrees that all faculty members are eligible for membership and that it will represent all faculty members equally. The board agrees not to discriminate against faculty members on the basis of race, color, creed, sex, national origin, marital status, or union membership. The bargaining unit may assume shared direction, with management, of affirmative-action programs.

Faculty Appointments. Legal authority for appointments rests with the board of trustees on recommendation of the president. Criteria for making faculty appointments are outlined, and the advisory role of faculty members within the department affected is delineated.

Non-Reappointment. If the administration fails to comply with any of the provisions of employment and probation, a non-tenured faculty member may appeal non-reappointment through the grievance process. Provisions may be made for notice of non-reappointment—with graduated schedules for when the notices must go out based on years of service to the institution. Also defined are reasons for which a non-tenured faculty member may be denied reappointment.

Dismissal. The reasons and procedures for dismissing tenured and probationary faculty members are set forth.

Procedures include notice and hearings, and specify what dismissals are subject to the grievance procedures.

Often the levels at which grievance procedures for dismissal are carried out are pegged to the grievant's years of service.

Dismissals occasioned by retrenchment are generally treated separately.

Retrenchment. Procedures are established for determining that a staff reduction is necessary, usually including consultation and budget review with the union or the faculty.

The order of layoffs is established. First steps include a request for voluntary layoffs, then enforcement of mandatory retirement. This is followed by layoffs of part-time faculty members, then full-time faculty in reverse order of seniority. The institution agrees to seek new employment for retrenched staff members.

Faculty members who have been laid off have first opportunity at any new positions created—without loss of seniority.

Provision is often made for staff retraining and for severance pay, possibly including continuation for a limited term beyond layoff of such fringe benefits as health insurance.

Occasionally, provision for parallel layoffs of proportionate amounts of teaching and non-teaching staff is included.

Promotion. The criteria for promotion—including years of teaching, earned degrees, and academic and scholarly contributions—are established. Procedures for promotion, such as notification of vacancy and process of application and appeal, are also determined.

Tenure. The waiting period for tenure generally is set at three to six years. General statements on tenure are often included as are specific guidelines on tenure privileges, criteria, and procedures.

A faculty committee is appointed to consider members eligible for tenure. The president recommends and the board of trustees grants tenure. Faculty members not granted tenure in their final probationary year must be informed in writing of the reasons for such denial.

Faculty Evaluation. Provisions for evaluation of probationary faculty members by departments, department chairmen, students, and administrators are stated.

Overload. Overload shall be voluntary. Teachers in the bargaining unit receive first consideration for extra assignments. Faculty members may receive extra pay for teaching extra students or extra classes.

Transfer Policy. Faculty members shall be transferred from one position to another only in areas of their competence.

The faculty members' preferences shall be honored wherever possible. Provision is made for retaining seniority in the event of a faculty member's transfer. Provision is also made for notice of involuntary transfers and for faculty application for transfers.

Transfers may be challenged through the grievance procedure.

Academic Provisions

Class Size. Responsibility is assigned for determining class size and for limits on class size.

Faculty members must give their consent to teach larger classes, and they are given extra pay for teaching larger classes.

Teaching Load. A faculty member shall not teach more than a certain number of credit hours per term or per year. Maximum total students per semester might also be stated.

Faculty members are not required to teach evening, summer, or Saturday classes.

Teaching assignments on any given day must be within a certain period of hours (usually 10).

Reduced loads may be provided for department chairman or for research and curriculum development.

Faculty Responsibilities. Responsibilities to the profession, to students, and to the institution are stated.

These responsibilities may include advising students, participating in general-faculty and departmental meetings, attending commencement, maintaining records of student attendance and academic performance, assisting in registration, meeting classes regularly, accepting a reasonable number of committee assignments, and participating in college-wide social, cultural, and professional activities.

Academic Freedom. Contracts may incorporate the *1940 Statement on Academic Freedom and Tenure* of the American Association of University Professors, statements developed by the American Association of State Colleges and Universities and the National Education Association, or a locally developed statement.

Academic freedom is generally extended to all instructional staff.

Compensation

Salaries. Main salary considerations include initial placement, advancement on the scale, rank-step scales, factors scales, and point systems.

Criteria for minimal placement on the salary scale are established, as are horizontal and vertical criteria for advancement.

Horizontal standards for salary advancement may include credit for professional improvement and further academic degrees, while vertical standards generally involve years of service to the institution and provisions for related work experience.

These, in turn, may be arranged into a formal rank-step schedule or into a factor scale, in which the base salary is multiplied by a factor based on degrees attained and years of service.

In a number of institutions salaries are further adjusted by a point system. Points are earned by performing duties in addition to full-time responsibilities.

Contracts may also include procedural provisions for length of the pay period (9, 10, or 12 months), methods of distributing paychecks, payroll deductions, scales for faculty members who do not fit any existing salary schedule, determining credit for prior experience, the signing of individual salary agreements, not spending for other purposes funds allocated for salaries, itemizing deductions on paycheck stubs, complying with the wage-price freeze, providing copies of the salary schedule to each faculty member, and payment for classes canceled for underenrollment.

Extra-Duty Compensation. In contracts not including a point system, specific extra compensation may be provided for overload teaching and preparations, extension courses, evening courses, correspondence courses, summer-school courses, registration, counseling, substituting for an absent colleague, research, curriculum studies, new courses, and each student over a set number.

The formula for payment may include regular salary, rank, seniority, or a flat rate.

Fringe Benefits

Insurance. The most common types of insurance provided for faculty members are auto (when fulfilling institutional responsibilities), dental, disability (short- and long-term), liability, life, major-medical and hospitalization, travel, and vision.

Leave. Types of leave include bereavement; child-care; court-required; maternity, paternity, and adoption; military; no-pay; personal; political and civil; professional; sabbatical; sick; and union.

Fee Remission. Those eligible to take courses without paying tuition and fees may include full-time faculty members, their spouses, and their children. They must meet normal entrance requirements for the institution and the courses, and the number of courses taken may be limited. At some institutions, full-time non-faculty employees are included in fee-remission programs.

Retirement Benefits. Retirement age and years of experience are set, and a choice is often given between a state retirement plan and TIAA-CREF.

Working Conditions

Professional Development Fund. A fund is established to allow faculty members to attend conferences, take graduate courses, travel, and otherwise develop their professional competence.

Clerical Assistance. Provision is made for the ratio of clerks and secretaries to faculty members and the procedures for their assignment.

Faculty Offices. Provisions include the number of faculty members assigned to an office (usually not more than two); specifications of furnishings; minimum square footage; and heating, cooling, and ventilation.

Travel. Where not included under professional development funding, provisions are made for who is eligible for travel funds, for what purposes, and what expenses shall be reimbursed.

Miscellany. Faculty lounge, holidays, parking facilities, medical services, funds for professional publications, computer services, air conditioning, and day-care centers are provided for.

FACULTY PROFESSIONAL ASSOCIATIONS

History and Collective Bargaining Policy

American Association of University Professors (AAUP). Founded in 1915 by a group of University professors, the AAUP has been the only organization that represents faculty exclusively. This professional association partially supported faculty collective bargaining first in 1966, when its Council voted "to authorize AAUP chapters to seek recognition as bargaining agents at institutions where effective faculty voice and adequate protection and promotion of faculty economic interests" did not exist. Three additional restrictions were imposed: a chapter must first obtain the approval of the AAUP general secretary; no strikes or work stoppages were to be called; and no agency shop arrangements were to be negotiated. This policy was buttressed by an additional statement, two years later, that conditions at particular institutions might be so unsatisfactory to the faculty that collective bargaining might be the best way to improve one's position. At the same time, the association suggested that faculties seek to strengthen the role of the faculty senate within the governance structure of their institutions. The AAUP Council, in 1971, announced that the association was to pursue collective bargaining "as a major additional means" of achieving the goals of the AAUP. This new policy was approved by the membership in 1972.

American Federation of Teachers (AFT). AFT was founded in 1916 to bring public school teachers into the American labor movement and

Staff Report of the Academic Collective Bargaining Information Service (ACBIS), reprinted by permission of the Academic Collective Bargaining Information Service (Orientation Paper #3, July 1975).

to win better salaries and working conditions for them. From the beginning it stressed an adversary relationship between school teachers and administrators. It agreed that teachers should join an organization independent of their employer and then attempt to use collective bargaining as the best way of improving their compensation and working conditions. Statutory rights to engage in collective bargaining were not really granted until the 1960's, however.

The AFT entered higher education as a labor organization before the NEA or AAUP, with the establishment of several locals for professors at urban universities during the 1930's. As a result, it was selected as a bargaining agent at those institutions which first elected bargaining agents.

National Education Association (NEA). Oldest of the three organizations, it traces its origins back to the National Teachers Association founded in 1857. Throughout most of its history, NEA's purpose has been to serve the professional interests of public school personnel—administrators as well as teachers. NEA became increasingly active as a political force at the local, state and federal levels. After 1945, it campaigned aggressively for the "cause of popular education" and, on behalf of its membership, for better "conditions of employment."

NEA became interested in higher education through its interest in teacher-training programs. This interest led to the formation of the American Association for Higher Education (AAHE). This affiliate, like the parent organization, accepted college administrators as well as professors. During the 1960's, the relationship between AAHE and NEA became increasingly troubled as NEA grew more teacher-oriented and advocated collective negotiations. The relationship between the two groups was terminated in 1968.

Internal organizational rearrangements within NEA resulted in the formation of a body called the Higher Education Association.

Membership

AAUP. Until 1972, eligibility for "active membership" was restricted to persons holding at least a one-year appointment to a position of at least half-time teaching and/or research, with the rank of instructor or its equivalent of faculty status, in an approved institution. This was changed in 1972 to include any professional appointee included in a collective representation unit with the faculty of an approved institution.

Of the three faculty associations, the AAUP has had its greatest relative membership strength in universities, numbering approximately 88,000 members. Its strength has been strongest among four-year, middle-tier schools. Among the academic disciplines, its strength lies in the social sciences and humanities.

AFT. Membership is open to any practitioner of the teaching profession, regardless of the level of instruction. Membership among higher education faculty is less than in the other two associations, numbering approximately 30,000. AFT adherents are said to be generally younger and more militant. They are principally in the social sciences and humanities, in two-year institutions. Recent election results indicate that AFT is gaining strength among faculty in four-year institutions.

NEA. Membership is open to any practitioner of the teaching profession whether at the elementary, secondary, or higher education level. In addition, NEA maintains that there is a single teaching profession operating at the local, state, and national levels and that the professional associations which operate at these levels are united in purpose, program, and association characteristics.

In higher education, NEA has a membership in excess of 50,000 faculty members, chiefly in two-year community and junior colleges. Its adherents in higher education are principally in education and other applied professional disciplines such as nursing and physical education.

Current Status

AAUP. Of its 33 current units, AAUP had the two-year Belleville Area College since 1967, added five in 1970, two in 1971, twelve in 1972 and five in early 1973. In Fall 1973, AAUP became the agent for two four-year institutions: Towson State College in Maryland and Wagner College in New York. More recently AAUP became the agent for, among others, Fairleigh Dickinson U. (N.J.), Hofstra (N.Y.), Boston U., Rutgers (N.J.), Regis College (Colo.), St. John's (N.Y.) and Temple (Pa.). AAUP's faculty membership nationwide is still the largest of the three agents. Although its traditional focus on four-year institutions is still the primary one, AAUP has four two-year colleges among its units.

AFT. Some twenty-one of AFT's 67 current units were organized by the end of 1969; seven were added in 1970, twelve in 1971, seven in 1972 and five in early 1973. The college division of the American Federation of Teachers represents academics at 67 institutions (17 four-year and 50 two-year), principally in states with strong labor movements. A merged AAUP-AFT unit represents Eastern Montana College.

NEA. NEA was the first of the organizations to enter collective negotiations, notably through community colleges. It has a large field staff and enjoys a base of over a million members within the public schools. Some forty of its 106 current higher education units were organized by the end of 1969; sixteen were added in 1970, twelve in 1971, sixteen in 1972, and five in 1973. New units in 1975 include St. Francis College (Pa.), Minnesota State Colleges, and Northern Montana College. NEA through merged affiliates with the AFT represents twenty institutions in the State of New York. NEA-AAUP represents U. of Hawaii. Of its 106 collective bargaining units, 24 are in four-year institutions, and the rest in community and junior colleges.

Experience with Faculty Contracts

AAUP. By July of 1975, AAUP affiliates had attained 25 contracts among its 34 units.

AFT. AFT affiliates currently have 52 contracts. Institutions in New York State formally [sic] with AFT or NEA and now affiliated with both, have 18 contracts among twenty institutions in July 1975.

NEA. NEA affiliates have some 90 contracts among its 106 institutions as of July 1975.

Goals for Academic Faculty

AAUP. The initial major task of this association was the protection of academic freedom in higher education. It has been involved with efforts to secure tenure, institutionalization of academic "due process," and the advancement of faculty salaries by fostering minimum standards. Some affiliated chapters also have pressed for faculty participation in university governance.

AFT. The AFT has been concerned primarily with improving the compensation and working conditions of teachers.

NEA. The NEA has been concerned with improving the position of teaching as a profession—by enhancing training, requiring more and better education, formalizing the requirements for teachers' credentials, etc. NEA's early efforts in higher education, like those at lower levels, were dedicated to improving the quality of education rather than the salaries or internal influence of teachers.

Increasingly, since the beginning of this century, NEA has attempted to improve the salaries and working conditions of classroom teachers.

Unit Determination Policy

AAUP. The make-up of faculty units varies greatly. In unit determination AAUP might attempt to follow these guidelines: deans, associate deans and others above a department chairman would be included *if* elected by faculty; if administration appointees, they would be excluded. The Association holds that a department chairman should serve "as the chief representative of his department within an institution." Broad principles of AAUP would seem to require it to favor inclusion of chairmen within the faculty bargaining unit under all circumstances. The chairman issue, as well as the other individuals included in the bargaining unit, in addition to professors, has varied from campus to campus. Unit determination, in effect, is finally decided at the local level. For example, Illinois' 110-member Belleville Area College unit, for which AAUP is agent, includes teachers, counselors, librarians, and department heads. At Rutgers University, 800 graduate assistants have been added to the original 2,500-member faculty unit.

AFT. The make-up of faculty units varies greatly and is determined at the local level. Generally speaking, in an AFT unit, department chairmen would be included, if possible, since it is felt that most do not have hiring and firing power. Deans, etc., who rank above department chairmen would be excluded. Also in the unit with the faculty would be found others who might be described as non-teaching professionals, i.e. librarians, student counselors, student placement officers. AFT may also include part-time faculty and lecturers. For example, Washington's Green River College unit includes 121 full-time and 191 part-time day and evening faculty members. Wayne County Community College has some 1,100 faculty on its payroll each academic year, including only 148 full-time professors. Many units, on the other hand, contain only full-time faculty.

NEA. The make-up of faculty units varies greatly and is determined at the local level. According to NEA officials the unit determination is generally left to the discretion of the state public employee relations board or comparable agency. As a result, NEA contracts might be negotiated with a unit which includes not only faculty but also department chairmen, part-time faculty, librarians, counselors, and other non-teaching professionals.

In fact, at Edmonds Community College and Everett Community College, members of a two-year college district, the presidents are also part of the bargaining unit, along with 170 full-time and 230 part-time academic staff, since they have a district director over them with whom compensation issues are negotiated. However, conceivably a contract might be negotiated with a "pure" unit comprised of only faculty members.

Faculty Senate Policy

AAUP. Firmly committed to maintaining and strengthening senates and other traditional arms of university governance.

AFT. Views differ from campus to campus. Some locals have tried to keep their faculty senates intact. Other union leaders have criticized senates as ineffective, slow-moving, and captives of college administrations.

NEA. Views differ from campus to campus. Some locals have tried to keep their faculty senates intact. Other union leaders have criticized senates as ineffective, slow-moving, and captives of college administrations.

Tenure Policy

AAUP. AAUP policy opposes strict numerical quotas on tenure but gives universities the option of "stricter standards for the awarding of tenure . . . over the years [that result in] consequent decreases in the probability of achieving tenure."

NEA. NEA maintains that:

"Every probationary staff member is eligible for and entitled to tenure upon reaching the prescribed level of competence. Hence, the practice of establishing institutional tenure quotas must be abolished. Such artificial barriers to the achievement of tenure are unrelated to any standard of professional competence and constitute a dismissal (i.e., non-renewal of contract) for arbitrary, capricious and frivolous reasons.

"The conferring of tenure on a staff member should carry with it a continuing contract of employment with the institution which is not annually renewed and can be terminated only for just cause. Just cause shall mean only flagrant and continuing failure to fulfill contract obligations without legitimate reasons.

"Whether probationary or tenured, a staff member whose employment with the institution is terminated should receive severance pay. The amount of this severance pay should be at least one-half year's salary for a second year teacher and should increase in proportion to the number of years of service the employee has performed at the institution."

Student Role

NEA. NEA opposes student participation be it as an active participant or just an observer.

Strikes and Work Stoppages

AAUP. It is the policy of the Association to call or support a faculty strike or other work stoppage "only in extraordinary situations which so flagrantly violate academic freedom or the principles of academic government, or which are so resistant to rational methods of discussion, persuasion, and conciliation, that faculty members may feel impelled to express their condemnation by withholding their services, either individually or in concert with others. It should be assumed that faculty members will exercise their right to strike only if they believe that another component of the institution (or a controlling agency of government, such as a legislature or governor) is inflexibly bent on a course which undermines an essential element of the educational process."

AFT. In 1960, the organization endorsed teacher strikes. Its policy holds that stopping work is a very last resort when all other means to bring about a fair settlement of a serious controversy have failed.

NEA. Prior to 1968, NEA's Representative Assembly opposed strikes and work stoppages, although many had been staged by NEA affiliates. In that year policy changed, since the NEA felt that it must support its affiliates on this issue.

Sources of Information on Collective Bargaining
in Higher Education

I. *Recent Major Bibliographies*

Coe, Allan C. "A Study of the Procedures Used in Collective Bargaining . . . ," *Journal of the College and University Personnel Association* 24:18–25 (September 1973).

Chaplan, Margaret A. "Collective Bargaining in Libraries: A Bibliography," in Frederick A. Schlipf, ed., *Collective Bargaining in Libraries*, p. 146–64. Urbana-Champaign: University of Illinois Graduate School of Library Science, 1975.

Education Commission of the States. *Collective Bargaining in Postsecondary Educational Institutions.* Report no. 45, p. 92–98. Denver: Education Commission of the States, 1974.

Marks, Kenneth E. *Collective Bargaining in U.S. Higher Education, 1960–1971.* Series in Bibliography, no. 1. Ames: Iowa State University Library, 1972.

Mortimer, Kenneth P., and G. Gregory Lozier. *Collective Bargaining: Implications for Governance.* Report no. 17. University Park: Pennsylvania State University, Center for the Study of Higher Education, 1972. This report contains a useful 12-page bibliography.

National Center for the Study of Collective Bargaining in Higher Education. Collective Bargaining in Higher Education series. New York: NCSCBHE, Baruch College, City University of New York.

Bibliography no. 1, comp. by John C. Allen, 1973.

Bibliography no. 2, comp. by John C. Allen, 1974.

158

Bibliography no. 3, comp. by Daniel J. Julius and John C. Allen, 1975.

Bibliography no. 4, comp. by Molly Garfin with Daniel J. Julius and Joseph M. Egan, 1976.

North, Joan D. *Collective Bargaining in Higher Education*. Bibliography no. 2. University: University of Alabama Manpower and Industrial Relations Institute, 1972.

Shulman, Carol H. *Collective Bargaining on Campus: Annotated Bibliography*. ERIC/Higher Education Clearinghouse Report no. 2. Washington, D.C.: American Association for Higher Education, 1972.

Tice, Terrence N. *Faculty Bargaining in the Seventies*, p. 345–81. Ann Arbor: University of Michigan Institute of Continuing Legal Education, 1973.

————. *Resources on Academic Bargaining and Governance*. Washington, D.C.: ERIC Clearinghouse on Higher Education for the Academic Collective Bargaining Information Service, 1974.

II. *Centers or Associations with Professional Staff and Research Faculties Working on Collective Bargaining in Higher Education*

These centers or associations perform various functions, such as publishing bibliographies and reports, compiling data, sponsoring conferences or research projects, providing literature searches, and generally acting as a reference or referral service. This list of centers and associations is drawn largely from the following publication: Education Commission of the States, *Collective Bargaining in Post-secondary Educational Institutions*, Report no. 45 (Denver: Education Commission of the States, 1974), p. 100–101.

Academic Collective Bargaining Information Service, 1818 R Street, N.W., Washington, D.C. 20009. Dennis Hull Blumer, Director. Telephone: (202) 387-3760.

The Service has an orientation packet which contains useful introductory material.

American Association of University Professors, Suite 500, One Dupont Circle, N.W., Washington, D.C. 20036. Woodley Osborne, Director of Collective Bargaining and Associate Counsel. Telephone: (202) 466-8050.

Publishes *Academe*, a newsletter.

American Federation of Teachers, 11 Dupont Circle, Washington, D.C. 20036. Robert M. Nielsen, Director, Department of Colleges and Universities. Telephone: (202) 797-4400.

Publishes *The American Teacher* and *On Campus*, a newsletter for its colleges and universities department.

Association of College and Research Libraries, American Library Association, 50 East Huron Street, Chicago, Ill. 60611. Beverly P. Lynch, Executive Secretary. Telephone: (312) 944-6780.

The ACRL office refers inquiries to Association officers and members who have experience relevant to the questions.

College and University Personnel Association, Suite 525, One Dupont Circle, N.W., Washington, D.C. 20036. R. Frank Mensel, Executive Director. Telephone: (202) 833-9080.

Education Commission of the States, Suite 300, 1860 Lincoln Street, Denver, Colo. 80203. Richard Millard, Director of Higher Education Services. Telephone: (303) 893-5200.

Industrial Relations Center, College of Business Administration, University of Hawaii, Honolulu, Hawaii 96822. John B. Ferguson, Director. Telephone: (808) 948-8132 or 948-8165.

Institute of Management and Labor Relations, Rutgers University, New Brunswick, N.J. 08903. James P. Begin, Director. Telephone: (609) 932-7480 or 448-8517.

National Association of College and University Attorneys, One Dupont Circle, N.W., Washington, D.C. 20036. Peter L. Wolff, Executive Director. Telephone: (202) 296-0207.

National Association of College and University Business Officers, Suite 510, One Dupont Circle, N.W., Washington, D.C. 20036. D. F. Finn, Executive Vice President. Telephone: (202) 296-2346.

National Center for Dispute Settlement of the American Arbitration Association, 1212 16th Street, N.W., Washington, D.C. 20036. Alfred E. Cowles, National Director. Telephone: (202) 628-1545.

National Center for the Study of Collective Bargaining in Higher Education, Baruch College, City College of the City University of New York, 17 Lexington Avenue, New York, N.Y. 10010. Maurice C. Benewitz, Director. Telephone: (202) 725-3131.

The Center's library offers computerized searches of current and expired faculty contracts. The system has full-text retrieval capability on search requests of any word in the contracts. The current cost for nonmembers is $150 per search of the active file. For more information, contact Molly Garfin, Librarian.

National Education Association, 1201 16th Street, N.W., Washington, D.C. 20036. Charles Bob Simpson, Manager of Higher Education. Telephone: (202) 833-4436.

Publishes *Higher Education Forum.*

Office of University Library Management Studies, Association of Research Libraries, 1527 New Hampshire Avenue, N.W., Washington, D.C. 20036. Duane Webster, Director. Telephone: (202) 232-8658.

The office offers a packet, called a SPEC KIT, which contains basic material on collective bargaining in libraries and on university faculty unionization. In operating SPEC (the Systems and Procedures Exchange Center), the Office serves as a reference point for guiding the inquirer to other sources of information.

III. *Journals, Newsletters, and Reporting Services with Frequent Articles on Bargaining in Higher Education*

This list is taken largely from the publication of the Education Commission of the States, cited earlier (ECS Report no. 45, p. 101–102).

American Association of University Professors Bulletin, American Association of University Professors, Washington, D.C.

Arbitration in the Schools, American Arbitration Association, New York. March 1, 1970, to date.

Change Magazine, Educational Change, Inc., New Rochelle, N.Y.

Chronicle of Higher Education, Washington, D.C.
Specific coverage on collective bargaining starts with 1969 edition.

College Counsel, National Association of College and University Attorneys, Washington, D.C.

College and University Business, McGraw-Hill Publications, Chicago, Ill.
Coverage of faculty bargaining in higher education starts in 1968.

College and University Reports, Commerce Clearinghouse, Chicago, Ill.

Community and Junior College Journal, American Association of Community and Junior Colleges, Washington, D.C.

Educational Record, American Council on Education, Washington, D.C.
Articles on unions in higher education start in 1968.

Government Employee Relations Report, Bureau of National Affairs, Washington, D.C.

Industrial and Labor Relations Review, New York State School of Industrial and Labor Relations, Ithaca, N.Y.

Industrial Relations, University of California, Institute of Industrial Relations, Berkeley, Calif.

Journal of Collective Negotiations in the Public Sector, Baywood Publishing Co., Farmingdale, N.Y.

Journal of College and University Law, National Association of College and University Attorneys, Washington, D.C.

Journal of the College and University Personnel Association, College and University Personnel Association, Washington, D.C.

Journal of Higher Education, Ohio State University, Columbus, Ohio.

Labor Arbitration Reports, Bureau of National Affairs, Washington, D.C.

Labor Relations, Bureau of National Affairs, Washington, D.C.

Labor Relations Reporter, Bureau of National Affairs, Washington, D.C.

Labor Relations Yearbook, Bureau of National Affairs, Washington, D.C.

Liberal Education, Association of American Colleges, Washington, D.C.

Monthly Labor Review, U.S. Department of Labor, Bureau of Labor Statistics, Washington, D.C.

Negotiations Research Digest, National Education Association, Washington, D.C.

Proceedings, Industrial Relations Research Association, University of Wisconsin, Madison, Wis.